The Forgotten Side of Bandelier

Archeology of the Tsankawi Ruins at Bandelier National Monument

Ryan Alexander Bloom

The Forgotten Side of Bandelier: Archeology of the Tsankawi Ruins at Bandelier National Monument

ISBN: 9781698971070

Cover image: The southern room block from its north side at Tsankawi Pueblo, this is the most intact portion of the pueblo with the highest remaining wall. All photographs by Ryan Alexander Bloom

Contents

Introduction

I currently reside in New Mexico, about 4 miles from Tsankawi and about 8 miles from Bandelier National Monument, but I am not a native of New Mexico. I moved here fairly recently, in fact. The history and culture of any particular place is hard for an outsider to absorb quickly, or ever understand fully, and I am no exception. Not knowing the true details of the lifestyle and culture of a locale means you never really quite belong to that place. Being born and raised in a given area is a good start, but having generations of relatives who lived the history of that place is the true mark of belonging. The Pueblo peoples of New Mexico definitively belong to the land they inhabit. With ancestors stretching back thousands of years before the Anglo-Americans, before the Spanish, before the Chacoan civilization, and before even the adoption of agriculture, they can lay claim to the Southwest region in the fullest sense. Trying to find a window into their experiences as a non-Puebloan is near to impossible, New Mexico born or not. This is also true for ethnographers, anthropologists, and archeologists that live, study, and work in the southwest. Even the most authoritative academic examinations of Pueblo culture, history, and prehistory by the foremost experts in the field are missing much of the meaning and context behind the simple facts. It is not that they haven't worked hard enough or done enough research, but that they haven't lived it. Most anthropological work suffers in this way.

I am a military brat, so I am not really a native of anywhere in particular. As a card-carrying member of the Choctaw Nation of Oklahoma, I am technically a "native" of America but have never lived in Oklahoma and my ancestry features plenty of European nations. In my defense, the Choctaws are not really from Oklahoma either. My Choctaw, or Chahta, ancestors walked the Trail of Tears from southern Louisiana and Mississippi, having been a part of the larger Mississippian Mound-Building culture of Cahokia fame, to Indian Territory (now known as Oklahoma). A forced march of over 500 miles. I have lived in Louisiana, but not as a cultural Choctaw. Even truly being immersed in the Southeastern woodland and swamp of the Mississippi Band of Choctaws would be a far cry from the experience of the Pueblo peoples in the arid southwest. My experience is quite different indeed. I was born in Maryland and have changed states every 3 to 5 years for most of my life, doing stints in Colorado, Virginia, Kansas, Louisiana, Colorado again, Washington, Colorado a third time, and now New Mexico. It is fascinating to look at the Pueblo peoples from my nomadic 21st century perspective and realize that the Acoma Pueblo, just west of Albuquerque, has been continuously inhabited since as early as 1144 CE. It is the oldest continuously inhabited town or city in the USA. To put that in perspective, the only Europeans who even had the foggiest idea that North America existed at the time of Acoma's founding were a few Norsemen who had a small and short-lived settlement in Newfoundland. The Byzantine Empire was fighting with the Seljuk Turks over Anatolia, the House of Wessex ruled England and spoke an Old English that was much closer to German or Frisian than our modern tongue, an Islamic caliphate controlled much of Spain, and the Song dynasty ruled China when Acoma was first settled. Through the conquest and colonization of the New World (the Acoma were conquered by the Spanish in the late 1500s), the Mexican Revolution, the Mexican-American War, and American Statehood in 1912, the Acoma Pueblo has persisted. That is an impressive run. I know a woman who is part Acoma and part Hopi from Oraibi. Located in Arizona, Oraibi or Orayvi is a Hopi village that is just a few years younger than Acoma. Founded in about 1150, it is the second oldest town in the USA. With ancestors in both the oldest and second oldest towns or villages in the country, her family may have the deepest and most unchanged roots of any American alive today! While she identifies as Hopi and is culturally immersed in both Hopi and Acoma ways, she lives a fairly normal modern American life. She works an hourly job, plays drum set in a Euro-American style band, and uses the Internet daily, essentially navigating 3 distinct cultures on a minute-by-minute basis.

Tsankawi was not as long-lived a settlement as Acoma Pueblo and, though it shares in the same traditions and background of the larger Puebloan culture, it is often overlooked as a footnote to the history of the region. If I had not bought a house a mere 4-minute drive from the ruins I would likely have overlooked them as well, which would have been unfortunate. While small and unassuming, they are quite densely packed with interesting features and captivating artwork. A single walk through the site arrested my attention enough to want to write about them. Flawed as my outsider understanding of the place might be, I think it is worth the effort to bring it to light. In order to even begin to appreciate Tsankawi, we must first understand its location in geological, prehistoric, historic, and modern contexts. The sense of place that we can grasp, small and incomplete as it will be as outsiders, is as important as the bare archeological facts of the site. In reality, the archeological facts of the site are quite few. In researching this book, I gathered resources on Bandelier National Monument and the larger Pajarito Plateau and looked for specific information on the Tsankawi site. A few resources had 5-10 pages of good information, a few others had just a page or two, and several failed to mention the site at all. A couple of the most egregious omissions went so far as to omit the site from contextual maps of the other nearby sites that were discussed. This dearth of consolidated information further spurred my interest in the ruins, not unlike how fans often rally behind the underdog in a sporting event. In a way, perhaps researching one small site in the area where I live, but do not belong, will help me connect and understand to a small extent. Maybe then I can share that with the world.

The larger and more impressive Chaco Canyon, Mesa Verde, Acoma Pueblo, and even Tyuonyi just down the road have had books, documentaries, theses, and dissertations made about them for decades. Thousands of pages and hours of film hang on their every detail. They are quite impressive, after all. Little Tsankawi (I say little, but Tsankawi had hundreds of masonry rooms in the main pueblo and over 300 nearby cliff dwellings) is rather charming in its own way and deserves at least one dedicated treatment. It is an official part of the National Monument after all, and a part that is deteriorating quite rapidly. Conservation of the site and its cultural resources is a serious issue that I'll touch upon briefly toward the end of the book.

Hopefully, with enough context, archeological information, and cultural connection to modern peoples, I can convince you too of the importance in remembering that Tsankawi exists and, further, how it plays into the broader scheme of a criminally underrated segment of North American antiquity and modernity. Tsankawi may not be currently inhabited, but descendants of the inhabitants live just a few miles away on a modern reservation. Ancestors of the inhabitants built the Great Houses of Chaco Canyon and stretch back to the last ice age. Tsankawi sits between the modern and the truly ancient, a window into a transitional period. In the best case, this book will be a small victory for a small village and will help outsiders understand and connect to New Mexico and the broader Pueblo culture to the small extent that we can. In the worst case, it will be an informational and hopefully interesting exploration of a singular ruined village.

Etymology, Demonyms, and Other Language Issues

One way to understand a culture or group of people is to examine their language or languages. I cannot speak any of the Pueblo languages, and there are some that no outsiders are allowed to learn, making an in-depth analysis particularly difficult. One thing we can do here is to look at the overall linguistic categorization of the tongues spoken in New Mexico and see just how they relate to one another. Another thing we can do is to trace the etymology of some basic place names and demonyms, or names for groups of people, and briefly look at the cultural issues and history surrounding some of them. In some cases the modern name or term for a place or group of people is a chain of unrelated or misapplied translations and often-inappropriate labels. The linguistic complexity should give you a sense of the amount of upheaval and number of competing groups that have made an appearance in the formation of modern New Mexico.

Modern Pueblo peoples and other Native Americans of New Mexico speak a variety of languages from differing language groups. Language is an integral part of culture and its correct or incorrect use and application can either serve to illuminate or obfuscate any particular anthropological issue. I'll be using a lot of native names and terms throughout the book and it is worth a look at the linguistics of New Mexico for general reference and as a way to discuss some of the relevant issues that surround languages and names. As unfamiliar names or terms come up throughout the book I'll try to define or translate them and give the language from which they come.

In 21st century New Mexico, English and Spanish are the most frequently spoken languages, however many Native American languages, both Pueblo and non-Pueblo, are also represented. Pueblo languages and dialects are usually split into 6 categories: Hopi, Keres, Tewa, Tiwa, Towa/Jemez, and Zuni. Non-Pueblo indigenous languages include Navajo, Mescalero Apache, and Jicarilla Apache. These 9 native languages can either be split into smaller dialects or grouped into the 5 large categories: Kiowa-Tanoan, Uto-Aztecan, Keresan, Zuni, and Athabaskan. The Kiowa-Tanoan family encompasses Tewa, Tiwa, and Towa/Jemez as well as other languages from the Midwest. Hopi is a member of the Uto-Aztecan family that also includes Nahuatl, the language of the Aztec empire, and the Numic languages of Colorado and Utah. Keres is the only member of the Keresan family, though there are several mutually intelligible dialects. Zuni is the only member of its family and, like Basque, has no known relatives. The Athabaskan family includes both versions of Apache and Navajo and is related to languages from Canada and Alaska.

Very broadly, it is assumed that direct descendants of the Chaco Culture speak languages in the first 4 language families: Kiowa-Tanoan, Uto-Aztecan, Keresan, and Zuni. Languages of the 5th category, Athabaskan, are spoken by peoples who moved into New Mexico either during or after the high point of Chaco civilization. The timeline and exact nature of the Athabaskans' relationship to the Puebloans is murky and up for academic debate. Of course, Spanish was added to the language mix in the 1500s and was used as the lingua franca until English came to the fore in the 1800s. Today, many Puebloan peoples speak English and their native language, but no longer use Spanish. Unfortunately, many tourists or newcomers to New Mexico attempt to converse with indigenous peoples in Spanish on first meeting, assuming that they are Latino or Chicano, leading to confusion and general miscommunication. Individual Pueblo groups have differing opinions on the teaching of their native languages. Some Pueblo groups actively teach their language to ensure its survival while others restrict the use of their language to Pueblo members and even forbid a written form. Modern pueblos to the immediate north of Tsankawi speak Tewa, while those to the immediate south speak Keres. We will explore the cultural and linguistic affiliations of the inhabitants a bit further in a later section.

The name Tsankawi is Tewa for "cactus sharp gap" or "gap of the sharp, round cactus" depending on whom you ask. Historically it was spelled Sankewi'i, Saekawi, Tsankawi'i, Sankewi, or Sankawi and like many place names in the region, variations in spelling are the result of a literate outsider attempting to fit the sound of the local spoken language into their foreign orthography. If the speller was Spanish speaking the resulting word is usually slightly different than if that speller was English speaking. Another example of variable cross-lingual orthography is name for the twin Spanish Peaks in nearby southern Colorado. Wahatoya, Huajatolla, and Guajatoyah are all accepted spellings for their original name. Realistically, since there is no written form of the original languages for many of these place names, any spelling that sounds remotely like the spoken word is as good as any other. Any spelling of Tsankawi is actually an abbreviation of the full name Sa'ekewikwaje Owingeh or sometimes Saekewikwaje onwikege, which is translated commonly as "village between two canyons at the clump of sharp cactus" or less commonly as "pueblo ruin above the gap of the sharp round cactus." There are a few more subtly different translations as well. Many Pueblos in the area use Owing-eh, (roughly synonymous with the Spanish pueblo or town) in the name, such as Ohkay Owingeh and Tesuque or Tetsuge Owingeh. All of the various translations for Tsankawi roughly indicate a village, a canyon, and a cactus. The specificity of these options is not terribly important.

Often, for convenience, the full translation in English is given for the abbreviated name, Tsankawi, which I find humorous. Various languages carry information at widely differing densities. Some require many syllables for simple ideas while others compactly fit large ideas into a few syllables. The difference in information density between Cantonese and English accounts for the extremely strange timing of the subtitles in old Hong Kong Kung Fu movies. Information density has limits, however, and it is a slightly comical stretch to assume that Tewa is able to represent a very descriptive 10-word English sentence in just 3 syllables. As unusual as the name Tsankawi sounds to Anglophone ears, with towns like Pojoaque or Powhoge, and Cuyamungue or Kuuy-emugeh just down the road, it is pretty typical for the surroundings and would not stand out if it were still an active village with a gas station or small casino. I'll continue to use the shortened name Tsankawi simply for ease and because this spelling and abbreviation is how the National Park Service officially labels the site.

While we are discussing spelling and foreign words we must touch on some demonyms, or names for groups of people, and the challenges or problems they pose. People that I will call variously Puebloans, Chacoans, native New Mexicans, original inhabitants, or indigenous peoples inhabited Tsankawi and the Pajarito Plateau. The antiquated terms for these people include Paleo-Indian for the ancient hunter-gatherer periods and Anasazi for the later agricultural village-bound civilization periods. Paleo-Indian is problematic in that the prefix paleo- meaning "ancient," was attached to Indian which is the misnomer for Native Americans that has persisted since the 1400s. Indian is the demonym for the people of the subcontinent of India. That too may have some colonial issues associated with it, but is outside of our scope here. It is obvious now, though it wasn't to Europeans in the 15th century, that America is a completely separate continent situated many thousands of miles from South Asia. Indian is not the correct term for any inhabitant of America, ancient or modern. Some Native American groups call themselves Indians and others avoid the term. In some cases it varies person to person. In Canada the most commonly heard collective name for aboriginal inhabitants is First Nations, though this is rarely applied to peoples from the rest of North America. The term Anasazi is Navajo, often translated as "ancient ones" or "ancient enemies." It is certainly not what the Tsankawi people (or Chacoan or other Puebloan peoples) would have called themselves and has sometimes been taken to be derogatory. Whether the term is acceptable in common use or in poor taste and to be avoided seems to oscillate through time. I'll avoid using both Paleo-Indian and Anasazi for the remainder of the book so as to remain on the safe side.

The name Navajo is derived from a reworking of the Tewa word navehu or "fields adjoining an arroyo." The Spanish incorrectly called the Navajo people the Apache de Navajó, which translates to "Apache of the fields adjoining an arroyo." To add another layer of confusion, Apache is also a contentious term because it is actually a culturally inappropriate French term for essentially any "ferocious" band of Native Americans. The Navajo and the Apache tribes are very closely related and both speak an Athabaskan language, but they are not a single group. So, referring to one group as a sub-variant of the other is not exactly right. The Apache originally called themselves Nde or Ndee meaning "the people," though they do often call themselves Apache today. The Navajo called themselves Dineh, Dine', or Diné, also meaning "the people," and many still use any one of those variants today. Nde and Dine' are effectively the same word if you just do a slight rearranging of the letters ± i, which is probably exactly what linguistically happened at some point in the Athabaskan past. We simply do not know what Chaco culture called itself, or what ancient peoples called themselves between the decline of the larger society in the 12th century and when the Spanish arrived in the 16th century. In historical times, the Pueblo peoples, all of which are descended from the Chaco Culture, or perhaps in some cases the closely related Mogollon or Hohokam cultures, can be grouped linguistically into the aforementioned groups Kiowa-Tanoan, Keres, Zuni, and Hopi, but can also be split further into individual Pueblos with distinct languages or dialects and cultures. The word pueblo is Spanish for "town" and is also a term applied from the outside, though one that seems to be fairly universally used to describe peoples who built large room blocks out of stone as the centerpieces of their villages. Because of this inherent ambiguity, I will use relatively vague or non-committal terms throughout the book to avoid the missteps of the clearly incorrect names of the past. I will use the terms Pueblo or Puebloan, which are descriptive and not terribly antagonistic, however not everyone is pleased with those, either. The Hopi, for one, find any Spanish language term used to describe them to be irksome.

Entrance to the Tsankawi section of Bandelier National Monument just off New Mexico Highway 4 at East Jemez Rd, looking east from the parking lot to Tsankawi Mesa.

Geography

At a basic level the name Tsankawi is merely a physical description of the village's location. A little background is necessary to fully picture the greater setting of that very specific location. Tsankawi is located on the eponymous Tsankawi Mesa about 35 miles northwest of Santa Fe, New Mexico near the town of Los Alamos. If that name sounds familiar it is because the Los Alamos National Laboratory was the home of the Manhattan Project that produced the first atomic bomb during World War II. At the time it was styled as the Los Alamos Scientific Laboratory. Nuclear research and many other scientific endeavors are still underway at the lab with around ten thousand employees on site daily. Many thousands of these employees pass by Tsankawi twice per day on their way to and from work. The modern trailhead for the ruin lies right at the intersection of East Jemez Road and New Mexico Highway 4. Jemez Road is designated as the official truck route into the lab and lab property lies just across the highway from the ruins. Lab property is home to many other archeological sites that are now restricted and only accessible by badged lab employees. Fortunately, Tsankawi is accessible to the general public because it is on the property of Bandelier National Monument. It is a bit of an oddity for the Monument, however, lying 12 miles north of the main body of the Monument in a detached enclave.

Anything north of Santa Fe is considered Northern New Mexico, so the ruin sits at the southern end of the northern portion of the state. Tsankawi is inside the nominal border of Santa Fe County though it is on National Monument property and surrounded by San Idelfonso Pueblo Reservation land, both of which are federally administered. Strangely, it is located about half way between Los Alamos and White Rock, adjacent to the primary road running between them. White Rock is a detached neighborhood of Los Alamos and not actually a separate town. Originally built in the 1940s to house lab employees, it was demolished completely in the 1950s and then reestablished in 1963 under the jurisdiction of the Los Alamos local government. Both portions of Los Alamos are located in Los Alamos County. The county borders here are quite irregular and one must drive through Santa Fe County and the San Idelfonso Reservation to travel by car between the two principle population centers, or major neighborhoods, of Los Alamos County. Los Alamos, Tsankawi, White Rock, and Bandelier all reside on the 300 square mile Pajarito Plateau, which in turn forms the eastern flank of the Valles Caldera.

The name Pajarito is Spanish for "little bird" and takes inspiration from the word Tsirege or "bird place" in Tewa. The Tshirege formation is a member of the tuff that comprises the bulk of the Pajarito Plateau and both the rock formation and the plateau (in Hispanicized Pajarito form) ultimately take their names from the ancient village of Tsirege, an archeological site near White Rock. The Tsirege ruin features the remains of a massive 800-room pueblo, many petroglyphs, and a long defensive wall. Located on Los Alamos National Laboratory property, Tsirege is not accessible to the general public except on rare occasion by guided tour. The contour of the long wall and the vague impressions of kivas and pit houses are visible from satellite images, which are the closest look non-badge-holders can usually get.

The Valles Caldera, or "Valleys Caldera," against which the Pajarito Plateau is located, is the gigantic collapsed dome of an extinct volcano that forms the core of the Jemez Mountains. The circular crater, representing the interior of the volcano, is one of the largest calderas in the world at a staggering 13.7 miles wide. It is easily visible in satellite or aerial photos and is one of the most prominent geological features in Northern New Mexico. Geologists have calculated that, when active, the Valles Caldera was rated 7 out of a possible 8 on the Volcanic Explosivity Index. This means that, while still quite impressive, it just misses the cutoff for being an actual supervolcano. 10,440-foot Pajarito Mountain and 10,495-foot Caballo Mountain, which together form the backdrop for the town of Los Alamos, are just high points along the rim of the ancient volcanic crater. At least 9 other prominences on the rim are named peaks with 3 additional mountains actually rising from

Above: The Sangre de Cristo mountains viewed from the northern edge of Tsankawi Mesa.

Below: The Valles Caldera (and Pajarito ski area) from the top of Tsankawi Mesa, Los Alamos National Laboratory buildings are visible on the adjacent mesa.

Looking across Los Alamos Canyon and NM 4 toward Tsankawi Mesa and the Sangre de Cristo mountains to the southeast. Part of Santa Fe is in the upper right corner at the horizon.

the floor of the caldera, called the Valle Grande, or "Large Valley." The largest of these 3 mountains is the conspicuous Redondo Peak at 11,258 feet above sea level with 2,454 feet of prominence above the crater floor. The volcano in total, with its rim of mountains, is over 20 miles wide and is home to the Valles Caldera National Preserve. The surface of the Pajarito Plateau is made primarily from a 300-foot deep deposit of material that was ejected from the volcano in 2 huge, successive eruptions. The numerous mesas were later cut by streams running off of the volcano and down through the deposits.

The Pajarito Plateau also forms the western rim of White Rock Canyon on the Rio Grande River, which flows through the Española Valley between the Jemez Mountains on the western side and the Sangre de Cristo Mountains on the eastern side. The Rio Grande runs past the base of the plateau at about 5,000 feet above sea level with the walls of White Rock Canyon rising abruptly up to around 6,000 feet. The plateau then slopes up in a series of stepped mesas to the town of Los Alamos, nestled next to the mountains at around 7,500 feet. The average elevation of the archeological sites on the plateau is around 6,000 feet above sea level though there are remains of ancient buildings in the town of Los Alamos and on the surrounding mesas above 7,000 feet.

Animal life is abundant on the plateau and would have been even more so in wetter ancient times. The area is home to larger game like elk and mule deer as well as smaller animals such as badgers, skunks, cottontail rabbits, chipmunks, wood rats, Abert squirrels, and mice. Down at the Rio Grande mink, otters, and beavers can be found. The profusion of prey supports predation from mountain lions, coyotes, foxes, bobcats, and black bears. Of course, with a name like Pajarito one would expect a considerable avian population. The plateau is home to many species of bird including robins, black-headed grosbeaks, hermit thrushes, warblers, vireos, western tanagers, crows, ravens, red tailed hawks, owls, eagles, a sizeable population of giant turkey vultures, and importantly to the ancient human inhabitants for their feathers, wild turkeys. Ducks and geese also migrate through the area seasonally. Rattlesnakes, bull snakes, lizards, and turtles are common as well as several varieties of beetle and spider, and even a small type of scorpion. Many of these animals were useful to the original residents and found their way into ancient artwork.

Driving to Tsankawi from Santa Fe is actually an interesting expedition in its own right. I'll describe the gist of the journey so that you can visualize the setting from a contemporary standpoint. Santa Fe is higher in elevation than Tsankawi and more than half the trip is downhill to the low point of the Rio Grande. Leaving Santa Fe on US 84/285 you first pass the very modern architecture of the Santa Fe Opera and the adjacent, brand new in 2018, Tesuque Casino. Tesuque Pueblo, built in 1694, is just off the road, though not visible without exiting. Tesuque Pueblo also owns the Camel Rock Casino just a bit farther down the road, named for a jutting roadside rock formation that looks conspicuously like the head and back of a camel. There is a small parking area for travellers who want pictures with the camel rock. Next you'll pass the Buffalo Thunder, and Cities of Gold casinos, run by the Pojoaque Pueblo in the towns of Cuyamungue and Pojoaque, respectively. Pojoaque was originally settled around the year 500 but was abandoned after the Pueblo Revolt in the 17th century, resettled in the early 18th century, abandoned again in the early 20th century due to an epidemic, and resettled most recently in the 1930s. As with many Native American reservations, the pueblos of Tesuque, Pojoaque, and nearby Santa Clara and Ohkay Owingeh, rely on the casinos to fund tribal services and spur their local economies.

The casinos and gas stations of Tesuque, Cuyamunge, and Pojoaque, with the exception of the newest casino near the opera house, are somewhat ironically constructed in the signature flat-roofed Santa Fe style. In modern architecture this is referred to as Pueblo Revival, a style that began in the 1920s and dominates the region. Pueblo Revival buildings imitate the thick squared adobe block and wooden beam construction of the ancient indigenous pueblos, albeit with modern European doors and windows. Recently, adobe has been replaced by concrete, cinderblock, or even wooden frame construction, however the earth-toned stucco exteriors are still styled to look vaguely like classic Pueblo Revival buildings. The irony is that the actual Pueblo people construct their commercial businesses in a contemporary western style that strives to emulate a 1920s style that in turn emulates their own prehistoric indigenous aesthetic. The nested derivations aside, it gives the Santa Fe area, and the highway corridor to Tsankawi, a very distinctive look.

Travelling northward, the Sange de Cristo Mountains tower above the highway on the eastern side with the Jemez Mountains running a little farther away to the west. The runs of the Ski Santa Fe resort are easily visible on the nearest mountain. The Rio Grande rift bottom has few tall trees so visibility is good across the valley. From a high point you can see many miles in every direction. It immediately clear that this landscape is very dry with exposed rock and dirt between small shrub-like trees and large branching cholla cacti. A friend from the temperate rainforests of Washington once remarked that she couldn't see any trees in the whole of the Southwest, just bushes of varying size. To an extent, she's right. Compared to the old growth forests and towering conifers of the Pacific Northwest, the trees of New Mexico are modest.

At Pojoaque you must turn left onto NM 502 in order to cross the valley and make your way onto the Pajarito Plateau. Continuing straight would take you past the 14th century Nambé Pueblo, a few miles east of the highway, into Española and ultimately toward Taos. 502 is an extremely wide and well maintained road that seems a bit out of place in an otherwise fairly rural area. It is the main artery into the Los Alamos National Lab and is therefore very heavily travelled by lab employees and maintained with lab access in mind. 502 takes you westward toward the Rio Grande, the Jemez Mountains, and Los Alamos. The plateau is actually built like a series of steps and from the approach in the valley it is easy to see the successive layers of brown, red, tan, and grey mesas and canyons sloping up to the Valles Caldera. As the road reaches its lowest point, at the river, you pass by the San Idelfonso Pueblo, established in about 1300, on the right, with the Santa Clara Pueblo, established around 1550, lying just a few miles farther north. None of the original masonry pueblos on the drive are actually visible from the road, unfortunately. You pass by their reservation lands and signs that point the way, but you'd have to make a detour to see the actual buildings. Most reservations are home to many more people than could actually live in the ancestral pueblo room blocks. And, of course, the pueblos do not have running water, heat, air conditioning, or any modern conveniences. Residents normally live in modern housing around the reservation, often with that ironic modern take on Pueblo Revival styling. If they have the means, Puebloans typically have a second home off of the reservation lands from which they can more easily access work, retail, food, and other conveniences.

At the Rio Grande River crossing you can look upstream, to the north, toward Española or downstream, to the south, into White Rock Canyon. The name White Rock is misleading because the nearby basaltic rock is actually quite dark. Similarly to the trees, the river looks fairly unimpressive here. Near its headwaters, the Rio Grande is quite narrow in comparison to the huge behemoth spans of iconic rivers like the Mississippi, Columbia, Missouri, or Ohio. Except during peak spring runoff, it would be easily possible to wade across the Rio Grande in many places without any need to swim. Along the banks there are stands of cottonwoods, willows, and box elders, which survive only by tapping into the abundant water supply of the river.

Upon crossing the river you begin the climb up onto the plateau passing outcrops of columnar basalt, and through many layers of Bandelier Tuff. Most of the upward climb passes through San Idelfonso land. The road flattens out at a fork where you can continue on 502 to Los Alamos up another steep mesa, known as the "main hill," or take a left onto NM 4 toward the neighborhood of White Rock (named for the canyon). At this junction several high cliffs surround the road on all sides with their many colored layers reaching hundreds of feet into the sky. The remains of cave dwellings and naturally weathered caves, which are sometimes hard to distinguish, are abundantly visible here. Just a quick mile or so on NM 4, with the relatively inconspicuous north side of Tsankawi mesa on your left, takes you right to the entrance of the Tsankawi section of Bandelier. Continuing past Tsankawi for another 4 miles would take you to White Rock and 8 miles further is the rest of Bandelier National Monument. Los Alamos is situated

on the highest set of mesas on the plateau with Tsankawi sitting
on what is essentially the second step in the staircase that is the
Pajarito Plateau. You could be forgiven for thinking that the area
was a true desert. Cacti and stunted piñon are abundant and, aside
from the river, there are no permanent sources of water. In reality,
precipitation does regularly fall on the plateau. The climate zone
for Los Alamos is confusingly called Coastal Temperate, even
though it is nowhere near a coast. It is about 900 miles to the Gulf
of Mexico and 800 miles to the Pacific Ocean. Despite the name,
average temperatures and rainfall totals determine the climate
zones, not their physical proximity to other areas with that zone
designation. Tsankawi, lower down the plateau, is in a semi-arid
zone and actually receives much less rain and snow. Of course,
streams run downhill, so the lower plateau benefits from the precipitation that falls at the top. Parking at Tsankawi is limited in
an undifferentiated gravel lot that segues fairly ambiguously from
the shoulder of the highway toward a short fence. Directly across
the highway is an inspection station for trucks wishing to enter the
National Laboratory, a juxtaposition of ancient and modern.

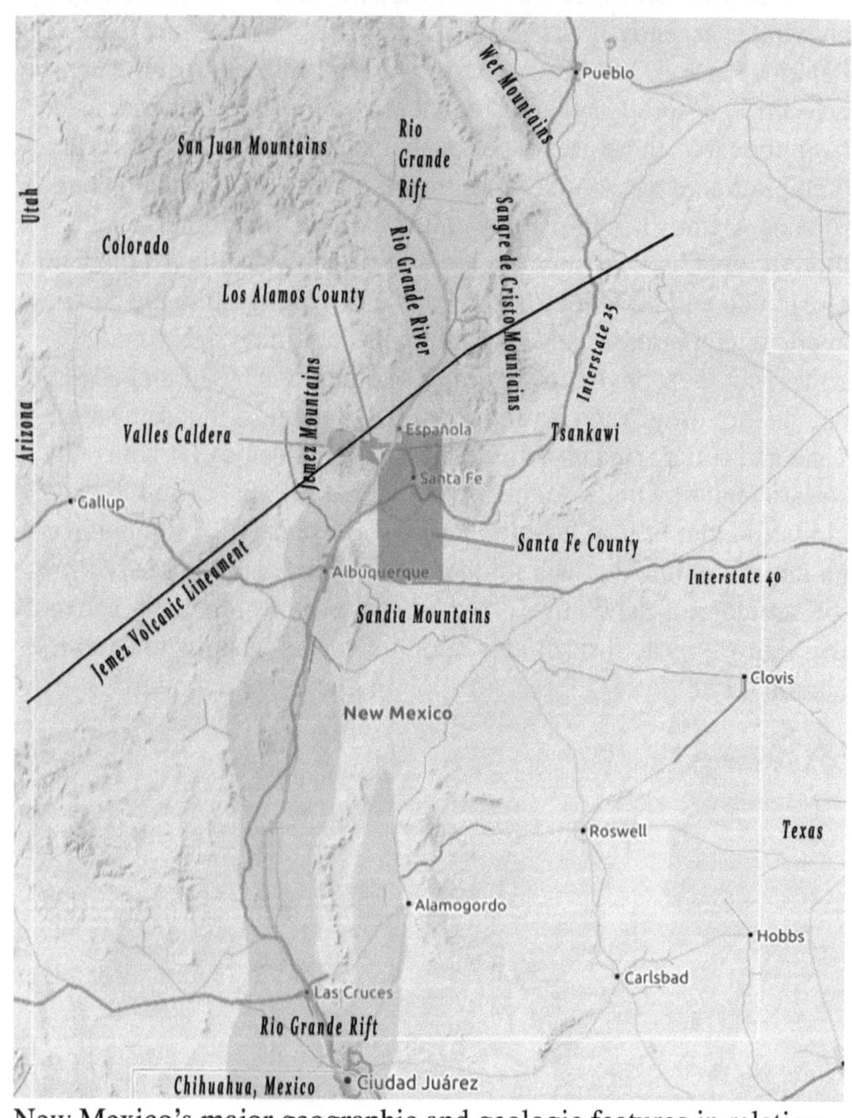

New Mexico's major geographic and geologic features in relation to Tsankawi and Los Alamos County.

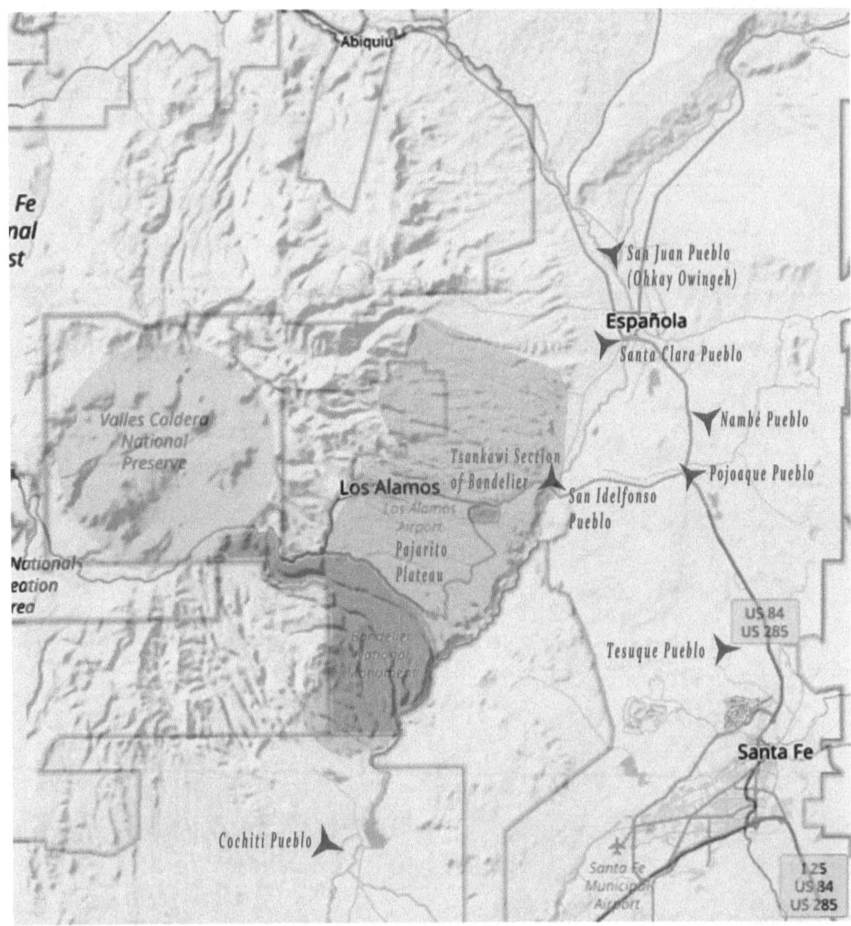

The Pajarito Plateau and the location of several modern Pueblos in the Northern Rio Grande region. Note how the caldera (large circle on the left side) is big enough to hold the entire city of Santa Fe.

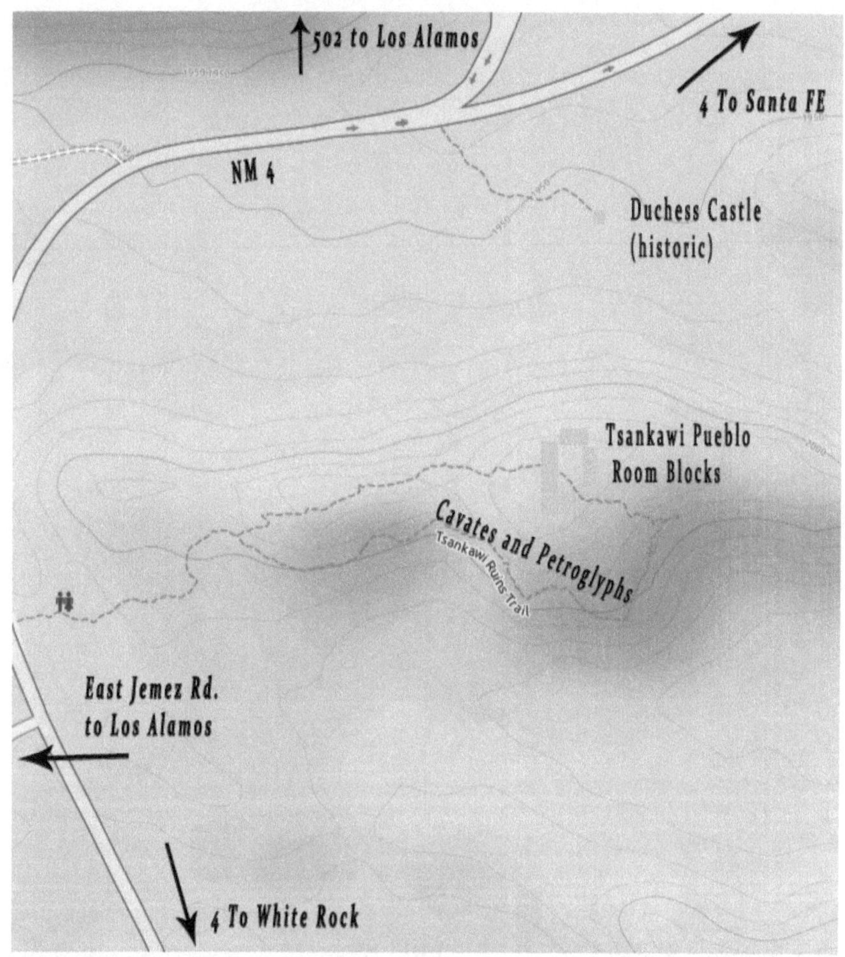

Topography of Tsankawi Mesa with the approximate location of the major room blocks.

Geology

The Rio Grande River roughly slices New Mexico in half north to south. From just after its headwaters in the San Juan Mountains of Colorado it travels from the San Louis Valley past Alamosa down into New Mexico and exits the state where the borders of New Mexico, Texas, and the Mexican state of Chihuahua converge. The reason it follows this path, and not any other, is that it follows the Rio Grande Rift, which is a cleft in the North American continental crust that has been opening up since about 30-35 million years ago. Similar rifts include the East African Rift Valley that runs from Ethiopia to Mozambique and the Gulf of California Rift Zone that is tearing Baja California from the rest of Mexico. The Rio Grande Rift is actively splitting the continent today and as the eastern and western halves of North America pull away from one another a depression is left between them. Low fault scarps from the rifting are visible in the sediment near Taos and some of these scarps are only 10,000 years old. A few thousand years ago is effectively the same as 5 minutes ago in geologic terms. The first humans arrived in New Mexico around 9000-10,000 BCE, meaning someone was definitely around to witness that specific Taos scarp activity. Many of New Mexico's most prominent and striking landforms are a direct result of the rifting process. The rift is also responsible for the many hot springs, such as Ojo Caliente, or "hot eye," that we humans are still enjoying today.

The Sangre de Cristo Mountains are some of the newest mountains in North America, raised during end of the Miocene just 5 million years ago. The Sangres begin at Poncha Springs, Colorado and sweep southward in a contiguous arc ending just south of Santa Fe. The highest point in New Mexico is found in the Sangres as well as the ski areas of Taos Ski Valley, Angelfire, Sipapu, and Ski Santa Fe. Their dramatic and abrupt western edge, which rises up 5,600 feet above the Taos plateau to a total elevation of 13,167 feet at Wheeler Peak, is the direct result of the subsidence of the land in the rift valley. The valley floor has dropped some 10,000 feet over the past 30 million years exposing the western face of the mountains by way of a normal fault at the base of the range. Of course, erosion and other factors have mitigated the height of the actual topography we see today. You can see evidence of normal faulting wherever there is a triangular facet at the base of a mountain, and most of the mountains in the Sangre de Cristo Range feature this telltale triangle. Over 100 miles of the Sangre de Cristo Mountains are clearly and dramatically visible across the valley from the vantage of Tsankawi.

On the western side of the rift are a series of volcanos, including the Valles Caldera of the Jemez Mountains. These volcanos are also a direct result of the Rio Grande Rift. The rift has split the continental crust deeply enough that crustal material can make its way down into the heat of the mantle and then rise again through the crust as magma to be erupted as volcanic lava. Coincidentally, New Mexico was also once located over a localized plume of magma called a hotspot. Hawai'i is located over a similar hotspot in the Pacific Ocean. Because the North American plate is moving as whole, this hotspot volcanism has drifted over time creating the Jemez Volcanic Lineament. A linear series of volcanic fields stretch from the Jemez Mountains northeast across the rift and toward Raton as well as southwest toward Mount Taylor. The Valles Caldera is exceptional in that it sits directly on the lineament and also tapped into the rift volcanism. Its aforementioned near-supervolcano status can be attributed to its position at the center of the crosshairs created by the lineament and the rift.

The Pajarito Plateau is made from volcanic tuff ejected from the Valles Caldera in 2 major explosive eruptions about 1.25 million years ago. Known as the Bandelier tuff, it is divided into 2 layers, corresponding to the 2 eruptions, the lower called Otowi and the upper called Tshirege. The explosions were similar to, but much larger than, the eruption of Washington's Mount Saint Helens in 1980. So large, in fact, that they caused the massive volcano to collapse in on itself, creating the Valle Grande in the center. There was once a crater lake, much like Crater Lake in Oregon, but it has since drained. Later, a large magma dome bubbled up inside the crater and created the interior mountains, including Redondo Peak.

The Bandelier tuff that resulted from the eruptions of the Valles Caldera is quite a soft rock and mountain streams quickly cut down through the tuff to the harder basaltic rocks below. The many mesas of the Pajarito Plateau, including the small mesa on which Tsankawi is perched, were a direct result of this process. Tsankawi sits on Tsankawi Mesa, of course, which is a high point between Los Alamos Canyon to the north and Sandia Canyon to the south. Both canyons drain into the Rio Grande River about 2km or 1.25 miles to the east.

The soft tuff of the mesas is easily worked by stone tools. The Frijoles Canyon sites in the main section of Bandelier, Tsankawi, Tsirege, Puye Cliffs, and many other archeological sites are located on the tuff of the Pajarito Plateau for several reasons, but a major reason is the workability of the tuff itself. The tuff facilitated the construction of cave dwellings, or cavates, the cutting of ladders, staircases, building blocks, deeply grooved walkways, and the digging of pit houses. Aside from the tuff, the volcanism produced deposits of obsidian, basalt, chert, and other materials suitable for the creation of cutting tools and there are several ancient mining sites on or near the plateau. Thanks directly to the geologic processes associated with the continental rifting, the inhabitants of the Pajarito plateau had, and actually still have, access to water from mountain streams and from the Rio Grande River, secure mesa-top and cliff-side building sites, easily worked stone for excavations, and a source of harder materials for stone tools. Los Alamos and the National Laboratory are located on the plateau for similar reasons, access to water and security being chief among them.

Regional Anthropology and Human Prehistory

Tsankawi Mesa had an active population for somewhere around 200-400 years. For comparison, the United States of America declared independence just 243 years ago (as of 2019). By that standard Tsankawi was a fairly long-lived and successful village. In a grander scheme, that time span is 3% or less of the total human story in New Mexico. Before we look specifically at a single village it will be immensely helpful to cover the prehistoric context of the region in broad strokes from the Pleistocene to the present.

Humans arrived in North America from Asia in the late Pleistocene Epoch, arguably around 20,000 years ago, but definitely by 17,000 years ago. Ice-age mammals like mammoths, giant sloths, cave bears, and dire wolves still roamed the continent. It was thought until fairly recently that the Clovis people were the oldest inhabitants of the Americas, with their distinctive stone points originally found (coincidentally) near Clovis, New Mexico. These points can be found all over the North American continent. Many sources will still cite the Clovis people as the first Americans because of a slightly flawed but seemingly logical connection between archeology and the climate. The oldest Clovis sites were dated to around 13,000 years ago and that date lines up conspicuously and conveniently with the fact that a land bridge, known as Beringia, connected Asia and North America from 16,000 to 11,000 years ago. The prevailing theory for many decades was that ancient Siberians crossed the land bridge on foot and dispersed throughout the Americas, bringing their Clovis-style technology with them. Some early Americans are likely to have done something like that, but in the past 10-15 years it has become clear, thanks to several new archeological finds, that human activity was taking place in North America much earlier. Human remains, stone tools, mammoth kill sites, and genetic evidence point toward the much earlier range of 17,000 to 20,000 years ago. These earlier arrivals would have likely used boats to cross from Siberia to Alaska, since there was no land bridge at the time, and then followed the coastline southward. Today, Alaska and Russia are only about 50 miles apart across the Bering Sea, and may have been closer at various points in the past depending on sea levels, making the journey difficult but feasible without any need for a land route. Some of these earliest Americans eventually made their way to what is now New Mexico.

As mentioned earlier, the first so-called "Paleo-Indians" arrived in New Mexico by at least 9000-10,000 BCE or around 12,000 years ago. These first New Mexicans would have traveled from campsite to campsite seasonally, collecting plants and hunting mega-fauna with stone-tipped lances in the famous Clovis style. From this point forward, for the next 5,000 years or so, bands of nomads periodically moved across the Pajarito Plateau, leaving behind stone tools and other small artifacts. Just as I was editing this book in mid-2019, the Los Alamos National Laboratory, in a slightly humorous episode, uncovered a cache of artifacts in its archives that date to around 10,000 years ago. They were collected in the 1970s by a staff archeologist, archived under the heading "Early Man," and promptly forgotten for 4 decades. These lab-owned artifacts include some Clovis points as well as other styles of stone tools. Eventually, the climate changed and the area became warmer and drier. The most impressive American mega-fauna like mammoths, sloths, camels, and other big game went extinct, taking many large predatory animals with them. The hunter-gatherers were then forced to change strategies and became much more vegetarian, essentially gatherer-hunters, relying on plants much more than animals for their daily nutrition. This shift, from hunting to plant gathering, marks the beginning of the Archaic Period.

The Archaic Period ran from around 6000 or 5000 BCE (depending on who you ask) to roughly 600-750 CE. During these many thousands of years the people of New Mexico gradually moved from a wide-ranging nomadic gatherer-hunter lifestyle to a sedentary plant gathering lifestyle with just occasional supplemental hunting. Following big game on seasonal migrations required vast territory, but gathering edible plants and processing them was best done in a smaller area. Somewhere between 5500 and 3500 BCE climate change caused bison, one of the few remaining mega-fauna, to disappear from New Mexico. The loss of such a lucrative game animal likely cemented the transition from a meat-based diet supplemented with plants to a mostly plant-based diet supplemented with meat. Accordingly, the range over which people moved decreased significantly.

Starting around 1500 BCE, Archaic New Mexicans began making woven baskets and are referred to by archeologists as Basketmakers. Toward the end of the Archaic, in the early centuries CE, the Basketmakers limited their seasonal movement to the point where they ultimately settled into villages. Archaic villages did not have the awe inspiring stone architecture of later periods, but instead featured groups of 6 to 8 examples of the more modest pit house. The Pajarito Plateau is littered with pit houses and Tsankawi actually has several of them, though at Tsankawi they were built much more recently than the Archaic.

Pit houses, as the name suggests, were partially sunk into the ground. A pit several feet deep would be dug and often lined with slabs of stone to seal out moisture and pests. Then, a squat wooden house would be constructed over the pit, packed with brush, and covered with earth or adobe. A single hole would be left in the roof to enter and exit the house and to provide a chimney for smoke. Ventilation shafts and auxiliary storage chambers were often dug around the main pit. The advantage of the pit house was that the earth provides great insulation. Even with the later invention of aboveground stone architecture, pit houses were still built and used because they could maintain a much more stable year-round temperature. In the winter they would be much warmer than the outside air, even without a fire, and in the summer they would be much cooler. According to data on some modern reconstructions, pit houses can maintain a temperature near 60 degrees in the cold of winter and the heat of summer alike. Pit house living would have been quite comfortable and a good buffer against the temperature extremes often encountered at Northern New Mexico's relatively high elevation.

Village-bound Basketmakers relied primarily on gathering edible plants from the surrounding area, supplemented with some small game hunting by way of stone-tipped darts launched from atlatls. The atlatl is a device common among ancient peoples that allowed a user to throw a spear or dart much harder and farther than by hand alone. Today, the closest analog of an atlatl is the plastic tennis-ball-throwing handle that dog-owners use to play fetch with their pets at the park. The simple stick with a cup for the ball allows the dog-owner to launch a tennis ball much farther than they could otherwise throw by extending the length of their arm by almost a factor of 2. An atlatl, at its core, used the same principle to lengthen the spear-throwers arm and gain an advantage in leverage and speed.

Easily harvested plants like piñon nuts and wild grasses were eaten along side difficult plants like yucca roots, which had to be dug up and processed heavily before consumption. There is some evidence that the early village-dwellers encouraged the growth of naturally occurring edible plants in almost farm-like concentrations. Some unusually dense stands of yucca plants, still visible around the Pajarito Plateau, are assumed to be man-made or at least man-encouraged. The latest Archaic Basketmakers made the transition into true farmers starting around 300 CE. They actively cultivated fields of natural crops along with a small-eared early variety of corn, introduced from Mexico, squashes, and gourds. Corn and squash farming was unequivocally agriculture, but was not as revolutionary for the Basketmakers as for some other cultures. Already living primarily in one place, they simply added farming to their normal routine of gathering and hunting. Essentially, they hedged their bets, not initially making a drastic lifestyle change.

Between 300 and 500 CE pottery was introduced from Mexico. Cookware that could withstand direct heating, as well as sturdy storage containers, were revolutionary to the ancient southwestern lifestyle and much more effective technologies than baskets. Cooking before the introduction of pottery was cumbersome. Since baskets cannot take direct heat, rocks would be heated in a fire and then transferred to a volume of water to cause it to boil. New rocks would constantly have to be heated and transferred throughout the cooking process to maintain hot water. The fires that heated the rocks were not very efficient and ancient peoples spent a lot of time and energy moving rocks around and collecting firewood to heat them. In contrast, durable and flameproof clay pots allowed for heat to be applied directly to the cooking vessel with smaller and more efficient fires. Time and energy previously wasted on collecting large amounts of firewood and transferring rocks back and forth could now be directed to other projects.

Around 600 CE beans were added to the agricultural repertoire from Mexico, completing the classic trio of corn, beans, and squash. These three plants, known as the three sisters, were cultivated together because the combination grows well together when interplanted in the same fields and helps keep the nitrogen level in the soil balanced. The tall corn stalks give the beans a natural lattice to climb, the beans fix nitrogen in the soil that the corn would otherwise deplete, and the squash leaves shade the ground to prevent moisture loss. Planting the trio was, and still is, a much more effective strategy for maximizing yield and balancing nutrients than the modern monocrop system we use today in industrial agriculture. This era was the height of Basketmaker culture. Armed with pottery and efficient agriculture, society began to advance fairly rapidly over the next 100-150 years. Pit house construction methods improved and aboveground storage rooms with open-sided work areas began to appear beside pit houses. Village sizes slightly increased, the bow and arrow supplanted the atlatl as the primary hunting weapon, and turkeys were domesticated.

By 700 or 750 CE the greater region transitioned into what is called the Pueblo Period. In the early Pueblo Period the rudimentary open, aboveground structures near pit houses evolved into fully enclosed jacal room blocks. Jacal is a type of waddle-and-daub construction where a thin wooden framework was covered with grasses and then coated with mud to form a solid structure. These enclosed room blocks were the first pueblos. Later in the Pueblo Period a special type of pit house split off from the standard residential model and evolved into the ceremonial kiva, which will be discussed later.

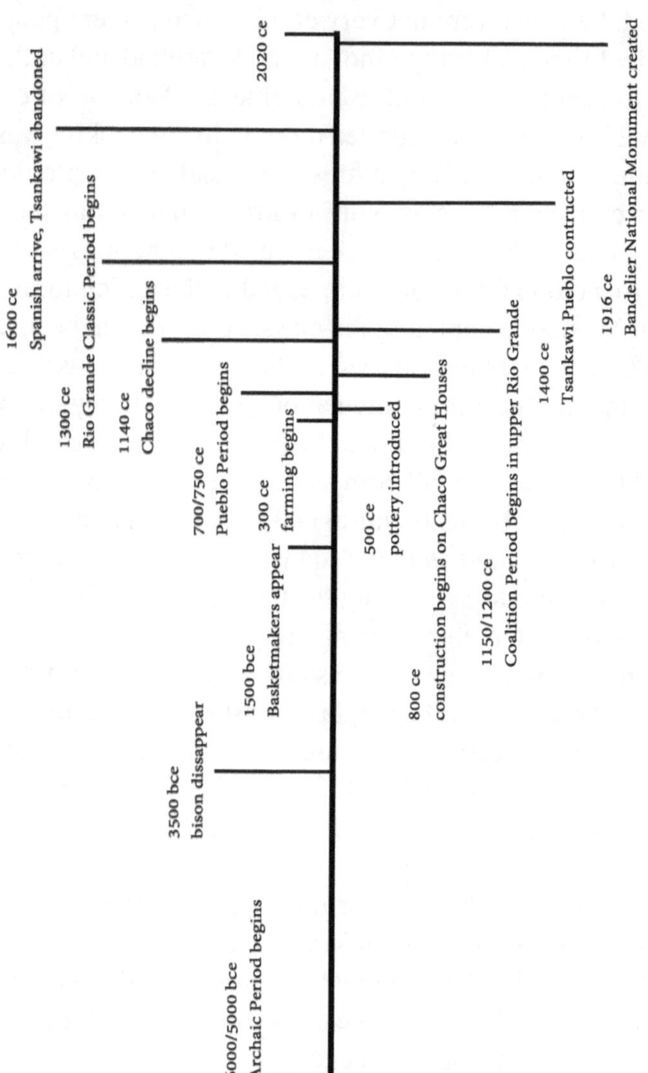

A rough timeline of events affecting the Pajarito Plateau from the Archaic Period to today.

At around the same time that early pueblo construction began, clay pottery completely replaced baskets for most tasks and corn farming almost entirely replaced foraging for the majority of people's diet. Archeologist David Stuart has suggested in his books that at the height of Pueblo corn farming people likely ate the equivalent of over 20 cobs of modern corn per day. Much of the corn consumed was not eaten off the cob but processed into meal on sandstone manos and metates and then made into any number of cornmeal-based foodstuffs. The mano and metate consist of a small handheld grinding stone, the mano, and a matching large flat stone work surface, the metate. It is a similar idea to a mortar and pestle. The first Archaic metates were actually stone outcrops and the work would be done in place with a convenient local mano stone wherever the geology naturally existed. When a group of people moved on from a campsite the mano was often left in the fixed metate to be returned to in the next seasonal migration period. Archeologists have actually found some manos resting in their immoveable outcrop metates, thousands of years after this practice was abandoned, just as their original users would have left them. Later, manos and metates were made from smaller, loose rocks that could be transported with their users as they moved around. The most advanced metates were shaped like bins, with sides to contain the corn meal. A well-equipped household would have several sets of differing grits from course to fine for exacting and efficient cornmeal production. Unfortunately, sediment from the stone grinding process wound up in the cornmeal and wore significantly on the teeth of corn-eaters, leading to major dental problems in large portions of the population during the eras of heaviest corn consumption.

The Pajarito Plateau was nearly devoid of human activity between 600 and 900 CE, from right around the transition from the Archaic Period to the Pueblo Period through the introduction of large masonry pueblos and Great Houses. This time span coincides almost exactly with the rise of the great Chaco Canyon culture to the west. It is theorized, though difficult to prove, that perhaps the original inhabitants of the Pajarito Plateau moved out to participate in the early stages of the Chacoan culture at other sites toward the end of the Archaic Period.

Chaco Canyon, the center of the accordingly named Chacoan Culture, is located about 140 miles west of Tsankawi and features some of the most impressive, if not the most impressive outright, examples of architecture in pre-European America. Quite frankly, the structures there are still impressive by today's standards. My explanation of Chaco society, architecture, and culture here is just the barest outline and I encourage you to research the subject further in order to understand the context of Tsankawi in more detail. While not entirely understood by scholars, the period of Chacoan supremacy is the defining era of Southwestern prehistory and essentially the classical antiquity of the region. In some ways, Chaco Canyon is to the Four Corners region as the Roman Empire is to Europe.

Chacoan society's most impressive projects were the Great Houses. Despite the name, they were combinations of administrative centers, religious and cultural gathering places, and storage warehouses as much or more than they were places of habitation. The numerous Great Houses scattered throughout Chaco Canyon had hundreds of rooms each and stood 4 or 5 stories tall in some cases. Pueblo Bonito, the flagship Great House of Chaco Canyon, covers an area of over 3 acres, had an estimated 800 rooms at its zenith, and featured walls up to 3 feet thick built of fine stone masonry. One of these Great Houses would be noteworthy for any prehistoric culture, but in and around Chaco Canyon there are at least 12 structures that qualify as Great Houses and up to 15 in the area depending on how define the boundaries of the Chaco core. The Great Houses are intermingled with many smaller pueblo structures and pit houses and thus Chaco Canyon would have been quite the metropolis to behold at its peak.

Great Houses were primarily built between 800 and 1140 CE and were the largest buildings north of Mexico until the 19th century. Upon their original discovery by Europeans, it was thought that the roughly contemporaneous Aztec Empire must have been responsible for any stone structures of Great House size during this period. While some Central Mexican objects and animal remains have been found in Chaco Canyon, likely acquired

The rear wall of the Pueblo Bonito ruins in Chaco Canyon with an interior kiva in the foreground. The walls still stand impressively high after more than 800 years without maintenance.

through extensive trading networks, no evidence of direct contact or immediate architectural influence from the Aztecs has ever been found. So far as archeologists can tell, Chaco builders were quite capable of designing and constructing Great Houses on their own without Aztec help.

The most amazing part of the Chacoan culture was that it wasn't merely confined to a single canyon. A relatively unified cultural and political Chocoan society covered a huge swath of the Four Corners region, including much of southern and southeastern Utah, a substantial portion of southwestern Colorado, a good chunk of northeastern Arizona, and most of northern and central New Mexico. In addition to the buildings of the Chaco Canyon area, additional Great Houses are scattered throughout the region, most numerously between Grants, NM and Cortez, CO, centered on the San Juan Basin. Some "Chaco outliers" include the Aztec and Salmon ruins in northwestern New Mexico, Far View House and Lowery Pueblo in southwestern Colorado, and Kin Ya'a in Southwestern NM. Thousands of Chaco cultural sites have been identified throughout the Four Corners area with perhaps up to 200 of these sites being Great Houses.

By some estimates 25,000 to 30,000 people might have lived in Chaco or a Chaco-influenced community in the early the 13th century. This is a comparable population size to the European cities of London, Naples, or Prague at the same time, yet at a much lower density. Many cities and towns of Medieval Europe did not have the architectural size and complexity that was standard for Chaco sites. For comparison, Charlemagne reigned during the early years of the Pueblo Period and the Viking Age of the North and Baltic Seas started at about the same time as the first Chaco Great Houses. Most Dark Age Western Europeans were subject to competing barbarian tribes and were governed by a system of feudal warlords. At its height, the Chacoan society had a vast trading network, an apparent "nationalized" system of food distribution and farming, a complex and advanced understanding of astronomy, and even a major road system (the usefulness and exact purpose of which has been debated). Though contemporary European technology was superior in some aspects, their political, cultural, and scientific organization was not.

Most Chacoans did not live in Great Houses, but in much smaller masonry room blocks or even in simple pit houses. Numerous typical "middle class" farms of the period had a complex with a small aboveground masonry building and several accompanying pit houses. Many times the masonry block was attached to a pit house, extending the back wall. It is thought that the aboveground section may have been primarily used for storage, rather than living space. Even at the castle-like Great Houses many of the hundreds of rooms appear to have been for corn storage, and not living or workspaces.

Of the thousands of Chaco era sites that have been found, many have masonry pueblos that are at least partially still standing up to 1200 years later, testifying to the quality of Chaco stonework. The finest examples of Chaco era construction, including most of those that are still significantly standing today, feature what is called coursed core-and-veneer masonry. The core would be constructed of rough stone blocks and mortared with adobe, often with integrated wooden beams for support. Around this core a veneer of smaller, finer stones would be built to provide stability and seal out the elements. This outer veneer usually had stones that were more rectangular and fit together tightly; rows or courses of larger stones would be alternated with tiny fragments of stone to fill the gaps, creating a very smooth exterior. Altogether the wall could be up to 3 feet thick and capable of supporting multiple stories of construction above. Many Chacoan buildings were constructed in bursts of activity spread over hundreds of years, though toward the end of Chaco supremacy some Great Houses, such as the one called Wijiji, were built in a single planned event. On a side note, Wijiji is a corruption of the Diné word Díwózhiishzhiin, meaning "black greasewood," but may hold the record for the most dotted letters in a row for any word in any language.

Another notable feature of Chaco era construction was the kiva. This subterranean room was typically circular, covered by a roof of wooden beams, and is thought to have been used for ceremonial purposes. All Great Houses have several accompanying Great Kivas and many smaller pueblos and masonry buildings have appropriate kivas for their population size. The kivas were essentially the same type of structure as a pit house, but larger and used for communal gatherings and rituals. It is thought that kivas were calibrated to the population and importance of a given site, with more and larger kivas in important and heavily populated areas.

Chaco culture thrived for around 350 years and then, most likely due to extended periods of drought in an already arid environment, and possibly due to warfare with another group of people, seems to have begun politically and economically collapsing rather abruptly in the middle of the 12th century. Stone pueblos and accompanying kivas have persisted as the village paradigm throughout the region up through the modern day, despite the deterioration of the unified Chaco cultural phenomenon. The Great Houses and the smaller lowland farming communities of the Chaco core are appear to have started losing population by 1130-1150. The Chacoans typically moved to higher ground seeking moisture and defensible positions as the society weakened. Notably, little evidence for a warrior class has been found at any Chaco cultural site. The few warrior burials that have been found date to very late in Chaco's reign as the dominant political power in the region. Mesa Verde in southwestern Colorado was inhabited throughout the Chaco period, but seems to have seen an influx of population just after Chaco society began to unravel. The largest cliff dwelling at Mesa Verde is the majestic Cliff Palace. Construction at Cliff Palace began, tellingly, in 1190 and most of it was completed in about 20 years, reflecting the need for secure living at higher elevations at this time. Cliff dwellings and upland pueblos of smaller scale became much more popular all over New Mexico and southern Colorado between 1100 and about 1250. It can be inferred from these broad events that Chaco was a relatively peaceful society. They did not appear to gain political power through force or maintain a warrior tradition, and their decline, though partially environmental, seems to have been hastened by a militarily superior aggressor. That aggressor has not been explicitly identified, though there is clear evidence of conflict in the immediate post-Chaco world. The upper Rio Grande region, including the Pajarito Plateau, experienced a surge in population in the 1200s following the droughts, violence, and decline of Chaco Canyon. The widespread move uphill and the subsequent years from 1150 to 1325 are called the Coalition Period in the upper Rio Grande. The Pajarito Plateau had been sparsely inhabited between 900 and 1200, but the Coalition period saw population gain which seems to have spurred village construction in the 1200s. Most Coalition Period construction on the Pajarito Plateau was on the mesa tops, and none of the structures were large or impressive projects. Waves of immigrants, often assumed to be refugees from other Chaco cultural areas, continued to arrive from about 1200 to 1325.

The Rio Grande Classic Period, beginning around 1300, was marked on the Pajarito Plateau by a move from the mesa tops into the canyon bottoms and the construction of larger stone pueblos. One large, canyon bottom pueblo, a flagship project for the era, is called Tyuonyi (perplexingly pronounced que-weh-nee) meaning "place of meeting" in Keres. The roughly circular Tyuonyi was once up to 3 stories tall and is one of the featured attractions in the main section of Bandelier National Monument today. The pueblo, located in Frijoles Canyon, was built and gradually remodeled over 150 years between 1350 and 1500. There are 245 ground floor rooms, with an unknown number of additional upper floor rooms that have unfortunately collapsed over the centuries. Several large kivas are located within the central plaza and around the outside of the room blocks.

The nearby Long House was another substantial piece of Classic Period canyon-bottom architecture. Over 800 feet long, it had several rows of adjoining rooms down its length and was up to 4 stories high. Situated at the base of the canyon wall, it is a good example of the type of cavate-based cliff-dwelling construction that was prevalent all over the plateau after about 1440. Remains of 353 rooms can be seen, hinting at a much higher possible number of rooms in its prime. The Frijoles Canyon village may have supported up to 500 people at its height in the 1400s. After about 1500 (some sources gives dates as late as 1550), most of the main section of Bandelier was abandoned. The population most likely moved south toward Cochiti Pueblo and other Keres-speaking villages. In contrast to the rest of Bandelier, the main structure at

Above: A large kiva at Chetro Ketl in Chaco Canyon. The interior stone structures may have originally been compartments beneath a raised floor. The entire kiva would have been covered with a wood and earth roof. For scale, the exterior walls are about 8-10 feet deep and the floor is maybe 20 yards across.

Below: The remains of Pueblo del Arroyo at Chaco Canyon. Note the thickness and smooth veneer on the walls.

Tsankawi was built on the mesa top rather than the canyon bottom. Tsankawi remained inhabited for around 50-100 years beyond the Frijoles Canyon village, up through about 1600. Its population likely moved north to the Tewa-speaking San Idelfonso or Santa Clara pueblos following a severe drought. Settlements at Puye and Potsuwi'i may have remained active into the late 1500s as well. The Tsirege ruin is the only settlement on the Pajarito Plateau thought to have been inhabited beyond the opening of the 17th century. No Spanish historical records indicate inhabited or active villages on the plateau, save for a single map from 1602, which shows the approximate location of an inhabited village labeled Messillas. Archeological evidence shows that Tsirege was likely the last village to be abandoned and thus may correspond to the village on the map.

Around 1580, the Spanish explorers arrived in Northern New Mexico and the historical era began. The first Spanish settlement in the upper Rio Grande area was built in 1598 and nearby Santa Fe was founded in 1607. Pueblo peoples were exploited and often violently forced to convert to Catholicism from their contact with the Spanish through the Pueblo Revolt of 1680, which is another topic worth researching further. The Spanish were temporarily driven from New Mexico (one of the few losses to indigenous people ever suffered by the Spanish) but returned and reconquered the area starting in 1692. The Spanish government ultimately issued land grants to many pueblos, which were essentially the precursors to the modern reservations. In 1824, Mexico broke away from Spain and took New Mexico with it, though the revolution was not very eventful so far north. When Texas seceded from Mexico in 1836 it nominally claimed much of New Mexico, though it did little to control the territory. In 1846, the US military seized the area during the Mexican-American War. New Mexico became a US Territory after the end of the war in 1848 and was granted statehood in 1912. According to the New Mexico Secretary of State, there are 23 officially recognized Native American tribes that live in the state. 21 of these tribes are Pueblos in the sense that they are Puebloan people and also that they still maintain their ancestral masonry pueblo buildings in their pre-Spanish locations.

There is one Tiwa-speaking pueblo located in Texas, Ysleta del Sur Pueblo, and the Hopi people maintain several pueblos on their ancestral mesas in Arizona.

A Brief History of Pajarito Plateau Archeology

Bandelier National Monument as a whole entered the official realm of documented archeology when it was "discovered" by untrained amateur "archeologist" Adolph Bandelier in 1880. Adolph was a banker from Illinois with no anthropological or archeological training, but through his efforts he did expose the numerous ruins of the Pajarito Plateau to the wider archeological world. He made his so-called discovery when he was explicitly shown the location of ruins at Frijoles Canyon by Juan Jose Montoya of Cochiti Pueblo who, along with all of the other Cochiti inhabitants, would have been readily aware of the ruins and their location for generations. Bandelier penned what is probably the most often repeated line about the Monument, "The grandest thing I ever saw." He went on to sketch and record the locations of 166 ruins in the area over the course of 18 months. He would return to the area for further exploration on 4 more occasions and, obviously, lend his name to the future National Monument. Bandelier's friend and fellow amateur Charles F. Lummis would also extensively visit the sites and write about them in the 1880s, eventually helping to found the School of American Research. Together, Bandelier and Lummis attracted more qualified experts to the area with their writings and promotional efforts. Bandelier is not known to have ever actually seen Tsankawi in person, but was the first to put its name in writing in a journal in 1885.

In 1899, Edgar Lee Hewett actually visited the Tsankawi mesa and sketched the ground plan of the pueblo, which he included in a 1904 publication. In 1902, a proposal was made to set up "Cliff Cities National Park" in order to preserve the ruins on the Pajarito Plateau. This park would have been much larger then the current Bandelier National Monument but it ran into opposition from livestock and timber interests in the area. In 1905, Hewett excavated two burial mounds near the pueblo and removed some

Above: The ruins of Tyuonyi in Frijoles Canyon with tourists for scale - only one of the several kivas is fully excavated.
Below: Long House in Frijoles Canyon - when inhabited this section would have been 3 stories high.

human remains, in poor condition, to the National Museum of Natural History's human skeletal collections (either 25, 28, 29, or 72 sets of remains were extracted and/or saved, sources differ on the specific number of remains and exactly where they ended up), publishing about them in 1938. He would also include content about Tsankawi in his publications in the 1940s and 1950s. It is unclear to this day exactly which mounds he excavated. One mound was almost certainly to the south of the pueblo, but the other is not explicitly identified in his publications and is subject to speculation. In the 1980s it would be reported that Hewett actually excavated 3 mounds, which only further confuses the issue. Hewett also excavated many other sites in the area and was the first to treat the Pajarito Plateau as a distinct cultural area.

In 1906 Theodore Roosevelt signed the Antiquities Act, which gave the president the power to create national monuments around sites with archeological importance. Hewett and other scientists campaigned to have what would become Bandelier protected under the act. National Geographic Magazine published an article with photographs by George Beam in 1909 that gave notoriety to the ruins around the plateau and in 1916 Woodrow Wilson officially created Bandelier National Monument. The Forest Service managed Bandelier until 1932 when control was shifted to the National Park Service where it remains today.

From 1931 to 1940, W.S. Stallings Jr. investigated several sites, including Tsankawi. His goal was to make a dendochronological record for the area. Dendochronology is a technique that uses tree rings to date archeological sites by comparing the sequences of rings in lumber, cut at the time of occupation or construction of the site, to a known and dated reference sequence. Temperature and precipitation fluctuations leave clearly visible evidence in the tree rings that can be read and dated for a given region. Dendochronology is one of the best indicators of the age of pueblo buildings because the wooden beams used to support the ceilings would have been cut at the time of construction from readily available nearby timber. The only major flaw in dendochronological dating is that older timbers were sometimes reused when a building was remodeled, confusing the timeline for construction. Tree rings combined with radio carbon dating of organic artifacts and comparative analysis of pottery styles, is what give us the approximate ages of various pueblos' construction and allows for a coherent timeline of prehistoric events.

H.P. Mera surveyed the site in 1935, primarily interested in Biscuit Ware pottery. His map of the Tsankawi village ruins directly conflicts with the information provided by Hewett. The Mera map leaves out many details, such as several kivas and other seemingly obvious structures. It does, however, provide accurate measurements of the included features and includes a new room block that Hewett's publications, oddly, did not. John F. Turney of the National Park Service also surveyed the site for pottery. In 1962, he collected samples from Otowi and Tsankawi that provided evidence for habitation before the construction of the pueblos, however his notes were apparently lost at some point before they could be published. In 1939, Robert H. Lister surveyed, mapped, and numbered 181 of the cavates on the mesa, stabilizing 120 of them, which in turn was the basis for an intensive cavate study by Wolcott Toll from 1986-1995.

From 1956 through the 1990s several proposals were put forward inside the Park Service to improve, develop, or reconstruct portions of Tsankawi Mesa with the intent of making in more accessible to visitors. None of these proposals were accepted or acted upon, which some archeologists see as extremely fortunate. Park Service "improvements" often reduce or eliminate the archeological value of an ancient site and Frijoles Canyon is given as a prime example of a site that has been diminished in quality by its accessibility.

By the mid- to late-1990s the gathering of new information about the site was in decline, but efforts to assess and conserve the ruin were gaining momentum. The Park Service reportedly began to see the lack of development at Tsankwai as an asset. In 1997, the University of Pennsylvania, the National Park Service, and San Idelfonso Pueblo organized a joint effort to implement an archeological conservation program for Tsankawi. Also in 1997, Nancy Olsen did an analysis of the abundant rock art. Michael Elliot completed a surface survey of the site in 1998 with the intention of gathering information that could be used for the preservation of cultural resources. The Elliot survey was only on 230 acres, a small portion of the nearly 800-acre Tsankawi Unit. In the early 2000s, Robert Powers mapped the site surface more accurately than previous attempts. Most recently, in 2008-2009 a team from the park service identified 355 cavates on the mesa, documented 316 of them, and assessed them for damage, drainage, and vandalism. 89 of the cavates assessed were not previously numbered or officially included in the previous cavate work of Toll or Lister and 13 of them were treated for graffiti or drainage issues.

Overall, very little of the site has actually been thoroughly investigated or excavated in an academic archeological setting and nothing has been reconstructed. What we know about the site comes from simple surface maps and non-invasive documentation, Hewett's excavation of human remains, the obviously visible petroglyphs and trails, and inferences drawn from other surrounding sites. The nearby and similar villages of Tsirege and Otowi have been more comprehensively excavated, lending data from which to make assumptions and inferences. Effectively, all of the work done in the past 20 years has been focused on preservation, conservation, mitigation of issues, or mapping to assist in future attempts at excavation or conservation. There are many unanswered questions and much left to be discovered.

TSANKAWI RUIN
THIS IMPORTANT RUIN AND THE CAVE ROOMS
IN THIS VICINITY ARE PROTECTED FOR FUTURE
SCIENTIFIC RESEARCH. PLEASE TAKE NOTHING
BUT PICTURES AND LEAVE NOTHING BUT TRACKS.
NOTICE

The Tsankawi Mesa Ruins

The area immediately around Tsankawi seems to have been inhabited throughout the Coalition and Classic Periods and right up through the arrival of the Spanish in the late 1500s. Habitation sites have been found near the Tsankawi village from the 1100-1200s, but construction on the mesa top Tsankawi Pueblo likely did not start until the 1400s, concurrent with the height of occupation in Frijoles Canyon and the Tyuonyi site. Unlike Tyuonyi, the inhabitants of Tsankawi did not abandon their village in the early 16th century. They remained in place for around another hundred years, when a severe drought may have forced them to relocate. Perched on top of a small, isolated mesa, somewhat remote from the rest of the sites in Bandelier, Tsankawi qualifies as a "veritable sky pueblo," according to Edgar Hewett, or a defensive pueblo site situated in a relatively inaccessible upland location. There are several other sites with even more difficult access scattered through New Mexico, Arizona, and Colorado including pueblos built atop giant boulders, on hogback or knife-edge ridges, and high atop steep-sided mesas. All of these defensible and relatively inaccessible structures appear to have been built in an uncertain and sometimes violent post-Chaco time frame from the 1200s through the 1400s.

The main pueblo at Tsankawi consists of 4 separate blocks of rooms arranged approximately in a rectangle. The rough rectilinear outline of the pueblo can be easily seen in aerial or satellite images, such as those from online mapping programs. The ground plan of the pueblo shows the outlines of around 200 rooms built from blocks of local tuff. It is thought that there may have been 300 to 400 rooms arranged up to 3 stories tall, but today none of the walls stand more than a few inches high. Depending on the accuracy of the size estimates, it may have had nearly as many rooms as Tyuonyi and would have been a fairly impressive structure in its prime.

Multiple cemeteries are located just outside the room

Above: Looking east from the western room block toward the Sangre de Cristo mountains with the foundations for walls in the foreground. The depression in the center indicates an unexcavated kiva that has filled with sediment.

Below: Looking northeast from the western room block toward the northern room block. Hand-cut tuff bricks in the foreground.

Looking south toward Santa Fe from the westernmost wall. The straight line of the foundation is visible center right but is obscured by fallen tuff blocks. Potsherds collected by "helpful" tourists (contrary to posted rules) can be seen piled in a rock in the fore-ground.

blocks of the pueblos on the mesa top. Two of the cemeteries (maybe 3, it is unclear if the mention of a third is factual), in the form of raised burial mounds, have been formally excavated, by Hewett, and are the only part of the upper mesa to be intensively investigated below the surface. Up to 72 sets of remains were removed from these mounds, again the number of remains excavated differs drastically from one source to another, along with pottery, tools, and other artifacts. On the Pajarito Plateau, burials were generally conducted in one of 5 ways: in narrow interior chambers that were subsequently walled off, under fireplaces that were subsequently plastered over, in ceramic urns, in cavate crypts, or in raised cemeteries. In all of these cases, the remains were laid in the fetal position, curled into a ball with the knees under the chin. The stretched out position favored by Europeans was introduced by Spanish Catholic missionaries and was rare to non-existent in prehistoric burials. The burial mounds at Tsankawi are an example of a classic raised cemetery burial and the remains were found in the normal burial position.

Bodies were wrapped with mats of yucca fiber or feathers and buried with utensils, tools, and pottery, often with a ceramic food bowl inverted on the head. No urn burials have been found at Tsankawi, but it has been suggested that a bowl on the head was a symbolic nod to the full-body urn burial used elsewhere. The cemetery mounds measure 50 to 100 feet in diameter and one mound contained about 40 sets of remains. The number of burial mounds, and the number of projected remains within them, do not account for the population size that would have lived and died at Tsankawi for the roughly 2 centuries of primary pueblo occupation. One proposal that solves this discrepancy states that the cemetery mounds were not a permanent resting place, but a temporary stop in a 2-stage burial process. Remains, according to the 2-stage proposal, would be buried in the cemetery mounds for some unknown length of time and then eventually disinterred and removed to another location for permanent burial. Under this theory a typical deceased individual would have been buried ceremonially in a cemetery mound immediately after death, with all the proper burial wares. After the appropriate period, the remains, along with

those of others in a similar time frame and burial strata, would
be disinterred and removed for a more permanent and less ornate
cavate crypt burial. A cavate room would be selected as the mortu-
ary crypt and the many remains would be relocated together for a
secondary burial, often without the ceremonially important trap-
pings of pottery, wrappings, and utensils. It appears that the bones
of many individuals were simply lumped together into mass graves
in cavate crypts once their time in the burial mounds was over. The
crypt cavate would then be sealed off. This cavate burial process is
commonly seen throughout the Pajarito area and the crypts generally feature the undifferentiated bones of many individuals.

Tsankawi mesa is though to have been home to a slightly
smaller population than the Tyuonyi/Long House village complex
of Frijoles Canyon, but was still a significant population center for
the plateau at its height. In addition to the aboveground structures,
there were 10 belowground kivas at the site, all of which have been
filled in with sediment over time. 2 were found in the courtyard
of the pueblo and the rest on the surrounding mesa top. They are
now only evidenced by shallow, vaguely circular depressions in
the ground. The remains of pit houses, similar in structure to kivas,
but smaller, have also been found. Kivas were important ritual or
ceremonial structures in ancient Puebloan society. At some Classic
period villages the proportion of pueblo rooms to kivas reached 70
rooms per kiva. At Tsankawi, the 10 kivas to the possible 300-400
rooms show a proportion of up to 40 rooms per kiva. At other sites,
kiva size dramatically increased over time allowing for more population per kiva. At Tsankawi, the kivas have not been fully excavated and their exact dimensions are unknown. The number of rooms
per kiva ratio is a proxy for calculating possible population size,
but without the exact size and construction details of a fully excavated kiva it is hard to make any exacting determinations about the
meaning of the ratio of rooms to kivas (or number of people per
kiva) at Tsankawi as compared to other sites.

Photos taken in the early 1900s reportedly show (I've
not been able to locate the older photos in any publication) that a
considerable amount of the deterioration of the site has occurred
within the past century. Much more of the pueblo stood in tact

around 100 years ago. The pueblo was constructed from the abundant soft volcanic tuff of the mesa. Stone blocks, hand-cut with harder stone tools, were stacked and mortared with adobe to create the room blocks. The Great Houses of Chaco Canyon used what is called coursed masonry, which alternates larger blocks with smaller filler stones in a smooth veneer around a core of larger, rougher sandstone blocks. Tsankawi's construction was not as elaborate, using only large rough blocks without a fine coursed veneer. Construction method, difference in the size of the structure, and the softness of the tuff, may have all contributed to why Tsankawi has collapsed nearly completely and older Chaco Great Houses still have portions standing.

The walls of Tsankawi, consistent with the style of many other pueblos, would have been plastered with mud or clay to seal them. While inhabited, the plaster would have needed constant repair and seasonal reapplication due to natural weathering and deterioration. Traditionally, the upkeep of the pueblo was a task allotted to female members of the community, along with child rearing and the tedious grinding of corn into meal with stone manos and metates. Once the plaster on this style of pueblo is left unattended, it begins to crack and weather away. After the village was abandoned, and the seasonal plaster maintenance ceased, wind, water, and gravity took their toll. The plaster deteriorated, then the adobe mortar weathered away, and finally the walls collapsed to the point that we see today. Many of the pueblos that are standing today in various monuments and parks were actually reconstructed from their original fallen materials by local Diné (Navajo) workers, in historical times, at the direction of archeologists. Reconstructed pueblos are only a best guess or estimate as to how the buildings originally looked. Talus House in Bandelier is an example of a cliff-side pueblo that was reassembled at the direction of modern researchers from nothing more than a pile of rubble, the original cliff-face boreholes for the vigas, or wooden ceiling beams, and the outline of the foundation. It may represent something like the original structure, or perhaps not. Reconstructions are also featured at Mesa Verde and other prominent southwest cultural attractions.

Along with the main pueblo room blocks on the mesa top,

Above: Talus House in Frijoles Canyon, a reconstruction of what a talus pueblo may have looked like - built in front of a cavate with wooden vigas supporting the roof.
Below: A series of cavates with rows of boreholes on the south face of a mesa adjacent to Tsankawi. Numerous examples can be seen all over the plateau.

Above: At least 15 cavates are visible here on Tsankawi Mesa along the main loop trail. A relatively recent rockfall can be seen in the center, probably obscuring even more dwellings.

Below: Cavates come in ovoid and rectangular varieties.

Above: Cavate interior petroglyph and chimney opening.
Below: A typical cavate room - the original plaster is visible on
the bottom third of the walls, the ceiling is black from smoke, and
there is a smaller cavity in the left wall. The light circle in the top
middle of the back wall is a socket for weaving apparatus.

Tsankawi villagers built numerous cliff dwellings, or talus pueblos, on the steep sides of the mesa. It is possible that, similarly to the Great Houses at Chaco Canyon, few people actually lived in the main pueblo and it was primarily used as a storehouse for food or for administrative purposes. A series of caves along the southern face of the mesa are all that is left of these cliff dwellings. Some of the caves, called cavates, may have been entirely natural, others started naturally and were augmented, and some were carved wholly from the tuff by stone tools. Tsankawi features 355 known cavates in small clusters. The boundary between the Tshirege and Otowi members of the Bandelier tuff is weak and most cavates were dug at this weak boundary, though there are cavates at multiple levels along the cliff faces. At Tsankawi, and nearby sites, the bulk of the stone tools found were made from chert, which is common in geologiocal deposits at the north end of the plateau. In contrast, the stone tools found in the main section of Bandelier are often made from basalt or obsidian, which are more common at the southern end of the plateau. The exception to this regional stone use was for arrowheads where both groups preferred obsidian to other materials. Interestingly, in the 1200s the use of basalt by northern residents was slightly more common, and by the 1300s it had declined to almost nothing, implying a subtle change in trade relations or travel to the southern end of the plateau and perhaps a change from a cooperative attitude toward a competitive one between the groups.

The cavates in the mesa cliffs represent the rear rooms of buildings that are referred to as talus pueblos (similar to the above mentioned Talus House reconstruction). Stone masonry dwellings, roofed and/or floored with wooden vigas would have been constructed in front of the caves, using the cliff face as the rear wall and primary support structure. By anchoring directly to the cliffs, talus pueblos could be anywhere from a single story to 4 stories tall. Not as impressive as the massive freestanding room blocks of the mesa-top pueblo, but still formidable constructions. With 355 known surviving cavates, talus pueblos would have been quite numerous on Tsankawi Mesa in its prime, turning the mesa's steep southern side into an apartment complex of sorts. The vigas that supported the roofs or the floors of upper stories protruded from sockets bored directly into the stone cliff face. Many of these sockets are still visible above their associated caves at Tsankawi and elsewhere throughout the plateau on many other cliff faces. Round, horizontally aligned sockets above a small cave entrance on a south-facing cliff are the telltale indicators of a past talus pueblo. These signs are easily recognizable on almost every mesa in the area. The masonry portions of almost all talus pueblos on the Pajarito Plateau have since completely collapsed and would not otherwise be identifiable as more than a pile of rocks.

This type of cliff dwelling was customarily constructed on the southern face of a mesa in order to take advantage of heat from the low-angle southern sunlight in the winter. Studies have shown that the ambient temperature of a dwelling built on the sunny south-facing flank of a mesa can be 10 or more degrees warmer in winter than one built on the canyon floor. In summer, when the angle of the sun is much higher, the cliff dwellings remain cooler than an exposed canyon floor dwelling because they have less surface area exposed to the sun. Talus pueblos also get a temperature mitigating benefit from their cavate rooms. Surrounded by tons of solid rock, the cavates are quite well insulated and maintain a steady temperature year round. Like pit houses, the cliff-side talus pueblos were carefully designed to keep their residents at a comfortable temperature in any season. They also had defensive benefits, only being approachable from one side, and often only after a climb. The insides of the cliff dwellings were often complex, with fire pits, chimneys, plastered interior walls, and interior petroglyphs. The chimneys would typically consist of holes bored through the tuff vertically in the ceiling of the cavate and accompanying vent holes can often be found near the floor. The walls and ceilings of many cavates still exhibit fire blackening from smoke and soot. Cavates could be used as dwellings, storage rooms, workrooms, or burial crypts, as discussed above. The remnants of loom anchors or sockets for other weaving apparatus have been found in a few cavates, showing that inhabitants sometimes used them as a space for weaving blankets or other textile items. Most cavate structures in Bandelier are thought to have been built in the mid 1400s through the early 1500s.

Like many other sites in the Classic Period, Tsankawi lies in the piñon-juniper woodland zone at about 6,600-6,700 feet, which is lower in elevation than the ponderosa forest zone that would have been typically favored in the earlier Coalition Period, but higher than the juniper grassland of the Española Valley below where several pueblo reservations are located today. The top of the mesa is actually not ideal for farming, due to its lack of water and poor soils, so the majority of the farmland for the Tsankawi village was situated in the surrounding canyon bottoms at around 6,000 feet. The canyon bottoms soils contained much more organic matter than those on the mesa top and would have been much more fertile. At the time of habitation, a permanent stream ran past the mesa that could have been used for irrigation and Tsankawi residents likely used the latest technologies to make best use of that water.

Over the centuries Puebloan farmers developed several innovative techniques to farm questionable areas. One technique was to use rocks to enclose a field, somewhat similarly to the terracing of fields found in Asia. The rocks would slow water runoff so that more would soak into the soil and make it to the roots of the plants. Another agricultural use for rocks was to space large cairns through the middle of fields. The rocks would accumulate moisture and shade some of the younger plants as well as retain heat through the night to warm the fields. Yet another rock-based technique was to cover the soil completely in a layer of cobbles after sowing the seeds. The cobbles would slow evaporation of water from the soil, prevent erosion of fertile soil, and would retain heat from the day well into the night, mitigating any surprise frosts and effectively lengthening the growing season. Some fields have been found with layers of cobbles several feet deep where the process of treating a field had been repeated for many successive growing seasons. The remains of many one- or two-room field houses can be found in prime farming areas around the mesa. These smaller sites are typically older than the Tsankawi Pueblo. In the era prior to the mesa-top construction of Tsankawi, families or small groups of families lived separately near their individual farms. When circumstances changed, the formerly loosely affiliated families grouped together into the communal, and defensible, Tsankawi village but retained their productive farmland in the canyons.

To ascend and descend the steep sides of the mesa, ladders and staircases were carved into the rock faces. Unlike our modern conception of stairs and ladders, these were note wide, flat steps or rungs. Instead, the steps were narrow gouges into the rock just wide enough for a single hand or foot. I have climbed some of these staircases and they are quite precarious, though the holds may be shallower now due to centuries of weathering than they were in their original condition. The Park Service has installed wooden ladders in places where steep climbs are necessary to navigate the ruins, for safety purposes. I suggest that visitors to the site use the ladders. The original staircases are only for the most sure-footed or those who are practiced in rock climbing. For the sake of liability I'll officially recommend: don't do it, use the park ladders. A fall from a cliffside staircase would be very unpleasant and possibly life threatening.

One of the most iconic features of the Tsankawi area is the abundance of deeply worn footpaths. These ancient trails are often referenced in books with no other mention of Tsankawi, and pictures of them commonly accompany descriptions of Bandelier. Similar trails exist throughout the Pajarito Plateau, but Tsankawi has the largest concentration of heavily worn and obvious foot-paths. A network of many different routes crisscrosses the mesa in several directions and the paths are worn up to 12 inches deep onto the solid rock. Made by centuries of foot traffic walking in single file, the paths were once at the surface, but have been ground down through use. Residents of the mesa walked either barefoot or in woven yucca-fiber sandals and trampled down the paths into the tuff simply by repeated usage. In some areas the paths are doubled or tripled, but each individual path is only wide enough for a single foot. Traveling on these paths is like walking a narrow balance beam but inverted. In some places you actually cannot fall down. The rock is too close at the sides to allow you to topple. When exactly these paths were started, or which ones are the oldest or youngest is nearly impossible to say. Modern foot traffic has

A characteristic trail at Tsankawi, worn several inches down into the tuff of the mesa from repetitive use.

worn significantly on the paths and parallel modern paths, worn in quickly by rugged modern boots, are nearly indistinguishable from original paths worn in centuries ago. It is quite the experience to walk the paths and know you are tracing the exact route, footfall by footfall in some cases, used by the original inhabitants.

Tsankawi's deep rock paths ultimately connect to a wider system of trails on the plateau. 173 segments of trails and paths have been officially studied on the plateau as a whole, with a total length of 11 kilometers. This is only a tiny fraction of the total trail system in the area, which may run up to hundreds of kilometers. Most of these trails are difficult to travel and study up close because of the modern issues of land ownership. Many groups manage the land of the plateau: the Forest Service, the Park Service, the Department of Energy, local pueblos, county governments, and private owners. A large portion of the land is part of the Los Alamos National Laboratory, which is very restrictive about access to its property for legitimate national security reasons. Tourists, spies, or trained archeologists alike wandering into radiation areas, firing ranges, explosive testing grounds, supercomputing facilities, or hazardous material disposal sites would be catastrophically bad for any number of reasons. Gaining permission to access to a segment of trail is often a logistical issue, dealing with several ownership entities.

Trails and paths are officially divided into 3 formal segments: local trails, major trails, and trail networks. The local residents, moving from mesa-top residences to water sources or farmland in the canyons, would have typically been the only people to use local trails. Major trails led from one pueblo to another and traversed the plateau widely, linking groups in the region. Some of these major routes are still extant and can be travelled easily, at least for a short distance. Others have faded with just small portions visible. The Old Pajarito Trail is one such major trail and it runs the length of the plateau for miles, connecting many major sites. Trail networks are a complicated division. They consist of many smaller trails, but are so closely spaced that they aren't separable as individual units. Tsankawi has 74 or more individual segments that are so close together that as a group they

A short staircase or ladder leading to a cavate on the cliff face.

represent a trail network with no main track. Many different uses, by many people, over a long period of time, during which priorities and needs for travel shifted, have contributed to the chaotic nature of trail networks. One modern issue with the trail network at Tsankawi is that trails used in the official Park Service loop around the site are being heavily worn in, while ancient trails are actively being filled with organic detritus and inorganic sediment. This obscures the archeological value of the trails and may contribute to the loss of some trails as they disappear back into the natural landscape.

Many of the major trails in the area, such as the North Mesa trail that runs past Tsankawi, use the tops of mesas as conduits for portions of their length, rather than solely running through the canyon floors as most modern roadways do. Researchers found this puzzling at first, but later realized that the canyon floor would have been covered with agricultural fields, homesteads, and other man-made obstacles. The tops of mesas, where farming was difficult, would have made better highways (literally) for ancient travellers. The North Staircase at Tsankawi, running down the north side of the mesa where there are relatively few other features, was an important piece of the village, for it connected the Tsankawi community with the North Mesa trail. In the post-Tsankawi era, the trails were still widely used by Puebloans from the Rio Grande valley in order to access the uplands for hunting. Some of the trails have pits dug across them, which were likely used to trap game. This would have been dangerous in the period when the Plateau was primarily inhabited, but after the populations moved out, it became an acceptable use of the trail system.

Most communities in Tsankawi's 15th to 16th century heyday had multiple, sometimes redundant, staircase accesses to their mesas from the trail system of the plateau. It is believed that an important feature of any village was its "Gateway Trail," or the official ceremonial entrance path. The staircase on the official Gateway Trail was often carved with more symbolic ritual intent, marked by more elaborate rock art, and revered as the actual formal entrance to the village, despite other heavily used access points. Construction of an official ceremonial staircase

This staircase leads 20-30 feet vertically up from a set of cavates on the cliffside to the flat top of the mesa. The steps have been eroded and are dangerous. The Park Service uses wooden ladders.

would sometimes occur after an adequate ordinary staircase had already been established for a particular route. The act of creating the staircase was as important as its use, so a redundant staircase carved with the appropriate ceremonial intent was required in some places. The important North Staircase of Tsankawi may be on its Gateway Trail, though it is slightly unclear. Gateway Trails often had "Guard Pueblos" nearby. One source I consulted points to the Duchess Castle remains as the Guard Pueblo for Tsankawi, which would make sense due to its proximity to the North Staircase and North Mesa trail. Although the source is relatively recent, it unfortunately quite confused. The Castle is actually the remains of a building from the historical period, built by a European baroness (and not a duchess, despite the commonly accepted name) as a school to teach skills to native community members such that they might be able to support themselves economically in a Euro-centric civilization. The fact that this was confused for a prehistoric pueblo in an archeological publication is slightly disturbing and creates confusion around the whole Gateway Trail issue for Tsankawi. The error may be partially due to the fact that the building was constructed of scavenged and repurposed blocks originally belonging to other collapsed pueblo ruins in the area. Duchess Castle is an interesting historical landmark, despite its lack of cultural connection with Tsankawi, and can be seen easily from the top of mesa

Duchess Castle, a historical ruin visible from Tsankawi Mesa.

near the Tsankawi ruins. A marker placed by the National Monument staff points it out from the top of Tsankawi Mesa.

Rock Art and Pottery

The people of the Tsankawi pueblo were skilled artists and artisans. Readily apparent at the site are hundreds of scattered pottery shards and many petroglyphs, or drawing carved into the rock. First, we should examine the pottery, as it is connects Tsankawi to a trade network and artisan production industry that was widespread across New Mexico and the surrounding areas as far back as the first few centuries CE. Pottery was introduced to New Mexico around 200 CE from Mexico. The earliest pots were called Sambrito Brown and examples survive from the 4th century. Ceramic making styles increased in complexity and decoration and diversified regionally over the following centuries. Pottery analysis is a very useful tool for archeology. The types of pottery found at an archeological site can indicated the age of the site, the associated culture or language group, and also the extent of the trading networks associated with the people who lived there. It is theorized that finely decorated ceramics were used as a currency of sorts in ancient times with some villages producing both simple wares for use at home and more ornate wares for trade. The tradable wares can be traced around the region, showing the extent of the networks where other goods were also flowing. During the Chaco society, trade was known to have extended hundreds or thousands of miles outside of the main Chaco region. Some Chacoan pots are remarkably similar in design to Aztec chocolate pots. Chemical analysis has confirmed that the Chacoans did indeed consume chocolate, which would have been imported from tropical regions in Central America. The Tsankawi inhabitants were immersed in the regional pottery making industry and there is a variant of Santa Fe Black and White named for Tsankawi.

Santa Fe Black and White pottery is associated most closely with Tewa speakers and glaze-painted pottery is more associated with Keres speakers. Tsankawi, known for its signature Black and White, is therefore associated with the Tewa ceramic tradition. Contrastingly, other parts of the Pajarito Plateau feature

A collection of potsherds arranged (by visitors) trailside on a tuff block. Several varieties of ceramics are represented here.

pottery styles that are more closely associated with Keres speakers to the south. We will discuss the cultural associations slightly more in depth in a later section. Regardless of the cultural or linguistic association, Black on White wares are the staple of Tsankawi and their shards can be seen everywhere. Also evident are examples of biscuit-ware, which succeed Black on White in the region. Tsankawi pottery was typically decorated, though some undecorated examples have been found. The decorations were generally geometric or abstractly motivic with very little in the way of representative artwork. There are reportedly no anthropomorphic pieces at Tsankawi and a scant few zoomorphic designs. A small number of pots were found with small bird forms and fewer still with lizard or turtle designs. The ceramic art at Tsankawi was high contrast and very bold with conventionalized design forms being used repeatedly over many pieces in a semi-industrial manner. Slight individual variation is present between examples, but overall the pots at Tsankawi mostly conform to a small set of basic geometric designs. Prehistoric pottery, with its many variations, gradations, and nuances of design, is a massive topic that underpins the majority of the archeological study of the Southwest. I have glossed over most of it here, but I suggest looking into it further on a wider scale if you are interested in the overall chronology of pottery styles or their wider regional distribution.

Rock art, or petroglyphs, can be seen all over the mesa at Tsankawi. Another consequence of the soft tuff, carving into the mesa with a hard stone tool, made from a material like basalt or chert, is extremely easy. Tsankawi residents took advantage of this and created a huge number of carvings around the pueblo by pecking or incising images into the rock. Many of the images are linear outlines of the subject, while a smaller portion are solid silhouettes of the subject in negative relief. Some carvings serve as trail markers, others appear to be ritualistic, folkloric, or astronomical/astrological. A vast array of differing forms and subject matter appear and, now that the pueblos and kivas have largely weathered away, the art is one of the most visually interesting features of the mesa. Nearly all of the surviving and visible artwork is carved into the south-facing cliff near the cavates. This may be coincidental to the

A triangular form in negative relief over a square grid-like form of pecked dots.

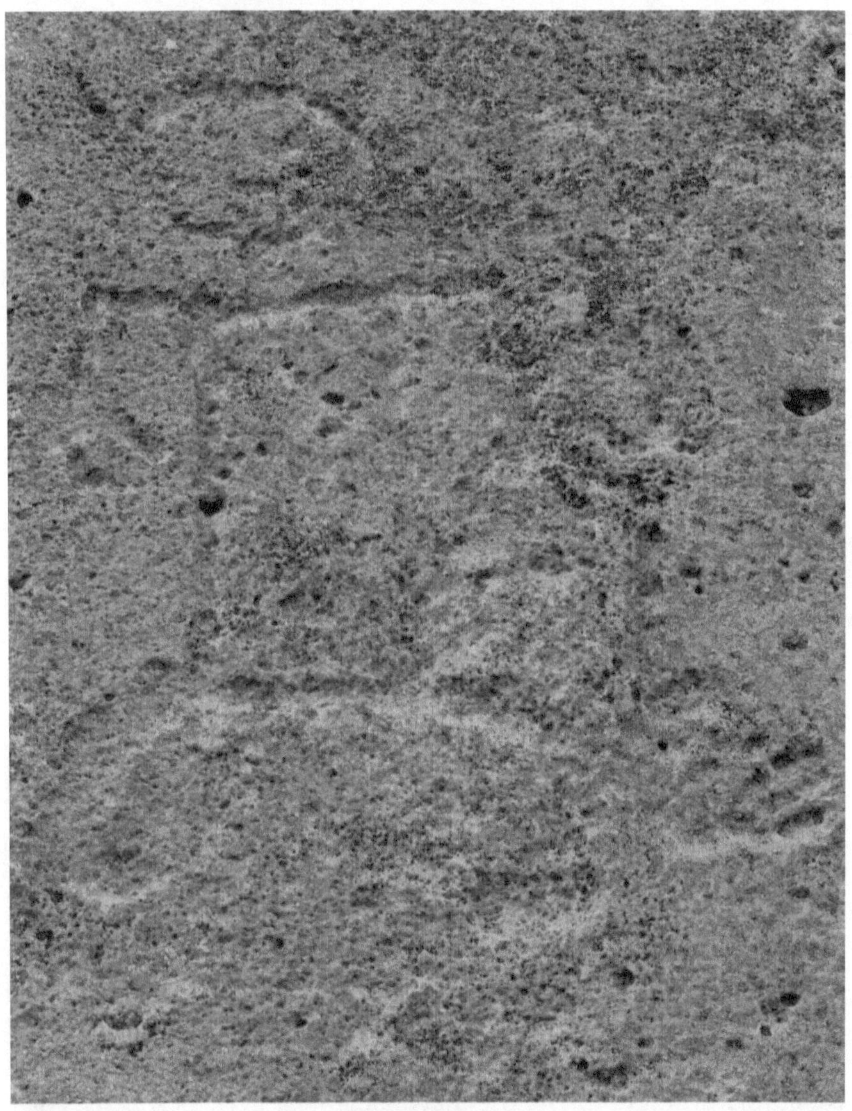

Humanoid figure with a rectangular body next to a set of concentric circles.

fact that all the cavates also face south, but the fact that only a tiny fraction of art is oriented to any other direction than south is indicative of perhaps a larger meaning. That meaning, if it exists, is unknown but speculated about and noted widely by experts. The included pictures of the petroglyphs at Tsankawi have been rendered in black and white in an attempt to make the image pop out more readily in the photograph. I have adjusted the contrast to allow the lines to appear most obviously against the rock background. The rocks on which the images are carved have been weathered heavily over the centuries and are covered in several colors of lichens. Some of the images are difficult to see clearly in person, even with the benefit of moving around to view them at different angles and in 3 dimensions. Photographs, even under ideal lighting conditions, rarely do the images justice. These photographs here should give you some idea of the forms or outlines, and a feel for the style, but are no substitute for seeing the petroglyphs in situ.

Some experts believe that the Puebloan petroglyphs of the Pajarito Plateau, which have a consistent style and a connection to the rock art at other sites, are part of a logical system of expression. Researchers compare them to Egyptian hieroglyphs or Chinese logograms, but at a more basic level of meaning. The petroglyphs do not appear to have a syntax, grammar, or linear semantic continuity, and thus are not exactly a system of writing in the sense of an alphabet or readable logographic text. They do have an internal consistency of style and a specific repertoire of images is used repeatedly in a clearly contextual way. There is evidence to support the idea that they carry some level of information somewhere between a purely aesthetic art form and a written language. For example, the repertoire of images that appear near water sources is entirely different than those that appear near agricultural sites or places of habitation. Pueblo petroglyphs are sometimes described as a mnemonic system or a form of graphic cultural memory. In other words, the images are a vague form of intentional communication but not specific enough to be considered a literal writing system. Most petroglyphs can only be interpreted along side the oral traditions and cultural understanding of the communities that made them. Hopi and Zuni petroglyphs have been studied exten-

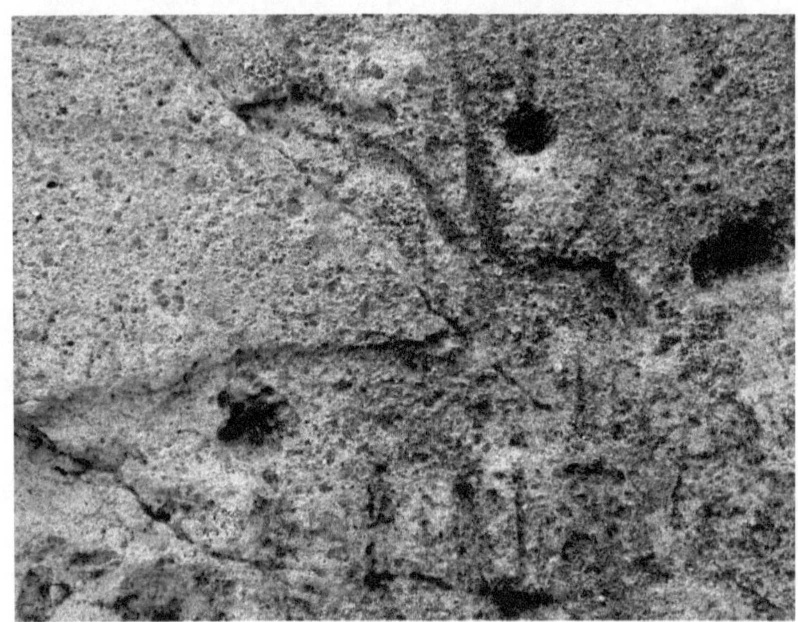

Above: A rabbit in negative relief.

Below: A set of concentric circles in the upper right
and a square in the lower left.

Above: An arrow in negative relief surrounded by linear and geometric forms.

Below: Several plant forms with a possibly a couple of Kachina figures.

sively and ethnographers appear to understand their rough meanings. For an abandoned community like Tsankawi, this level of understanding is currently impossible due to the absence of direct cultural context.

It was only recently that researchers even considered the idea that the petroglyphs could have a meaning at all. Hewett, for all his contributions, was a bit shortsighted. He called the petroglyphs, "idle picture making." Similarly, for a large portion of the history of Maya archeology in Mesoamerica, the Maya writing system was viewed under the assumption that it was vaguely representative art, rather than a readable language. It took quite a bit of effort in the 20th century to change the perceptions of the mainstream archeological community and even consider that the characters might be syllabic and translatable into readable text. We now know that Maya characters are a specific written language that can be directly translated and read in a systematic way. Pueblo petroglyphs are unlikely to yield a coherent writing system like the Maya language, but they are certainly more than idle pictures. Unfortunately, the establishment is still adjusting to that viewpoint. Even researchers who look at Pueblo art seriously often focus extensively on comparative morphology out of context, or essentially looking at the similar images from different sites side-by-side. This would be akin to looking at samples of handwriting for the way the letters are shaped, but without reading the words. Of course, there are no words that anyone has been able to detect, but there is a context. An effort to assign a taxonomy to the images with stylistic labels and a rough chronology has been undertaken, but with little success. Dating the images is difficult and they do not adhere to the strict "manufacturing" conventions that are valuable in pottery style analysis. A true cultural "reading" of the petroglyphs in context, similarly to those of the Zuni or Hopi, is difficult to impossible at the present. Unfortunately, it is also the most appropriate way to view them, in contrast to a purely morphological or taxonomic view, which discards context. The scientific community still appears to be working on this problem.

Many of the petroglyphs at Tsankawi are images of Kachina or Kachina-like entities. Kachina are spirits or otherworldly per-

Above: Several humanoid figures with adjacent crosses, circles, and other small forms.

Below: An animal form, perhaps a roadrunner?

Above: Several humanoid figures.

Below: A couple of triangular forms in negative relief.

sonifications of different objects, phenomena, locations, or ideas. The word Kachina or Kacina is of Keres origin and simply means "supernatural." There are countless Kachina who are associated with things such as rain, the sun, the moon, birds, animals, plants, the harvest, specific foods, and more. They have complex backstories and relationships, as with any pantheon, that play out in, art, dance, and stories. Anthropologists do not know the names of all the Kachina and are unsure of even how many exist or what many of their functions are. Not all Puebloan communities are forthcoming with outsiders as to their ritual practices. The Zuni, for example, are secretive with some of their ceremonies and generally do not believe they should be exploited by sharing them in public. We do know that Kachina are not gods in the sense that European theology would recognize, but are supernatural beings to be respected, nonetheless.

There are several slightly different interpretations of these spirit entities between different Puebloan groups, with a few differing origin stories, but the pueblos also share many similarities in their representations and the traditions surrounding them. Kachina dolls and costumed ceremonial dancers are commonly used to represent the spirits of dozens (at least) of different supernatural entities. It is unclear when Kachina became important to the Pueblo peoples, but one theory suggests that they rose to prominence after the downfall of the Chacoan society. According to the theory, the sudden collapse of the Chaco Great House way of life suggested to subsequent generations of people that whatever rituals or ceremonies were used at the Chaco zenith were now ineffective for ensuring good luck, adequate harvests, and peace. In the place of the Chaco ritual repertoire, Kachina rose to a much more prominent role in spiritual practice. Whether this theory is in any way accurate is probably impossible to say with certainty. It should be taken as simply one possible suggestion. Scholars mostly agree that however this form of worship came into fashion, it was imported to the Rio Grande region from the Zuni areas or even further west. From the rock art we can tell that Kachina had arrived on the Pajarito Plateau by the Classic period at the absolute latest, but were probably part of the culture much earlier.

Above: A Kokopelli figure in profile, facing right, with traditonal flute and humped back.

Below: A bird-like form in negative relief.

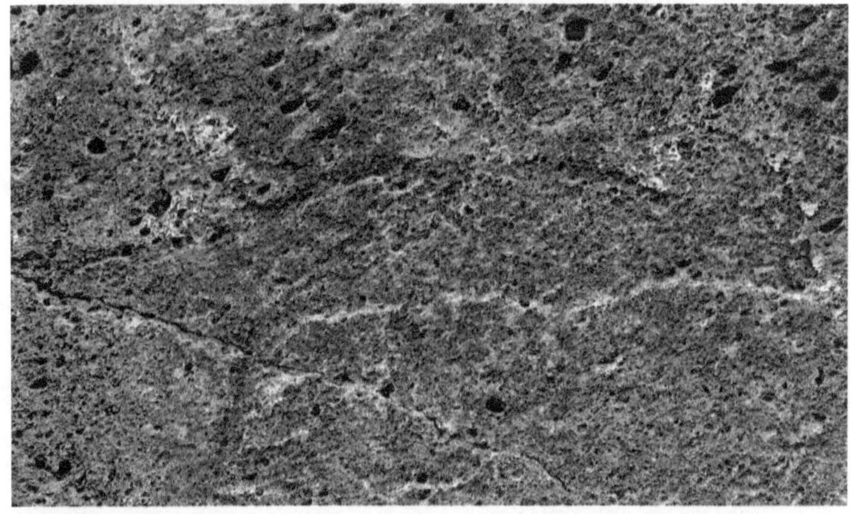

At Tsankawi, many of the Kachina carvings are unidentified and researchers are unable correlate them with a known modern example. Despite this, their forms are obviously meant to represent a supernatural entity and not a human or animal. A few, such as the Squash Kachina, Corn Dancer Kachina, and the common Kokopelli flute player, are clearly recognizable. The name Kokopelli is the Hopi name, meaning "Kachina hump," for what is a nearly ubiquitous figure in the southwest. Kokopelli is a humpbacked humanoid figure, always shown in profile, who appears to be playing a flute. Americanized Kokopelli figures often adorn "southwestern" themed items like lampshades, light switch covers, mailboxes, wall hangings, throw pillows, and other modern American items wishing to appear authentically New Mexican or Arizonian. You have undoubtedly seen an item like this if you have ever visited the southwest region.

Animals appear frequently in the rock artwork including dogs, elk, deer, birds, snakes, and even seemingly imaginary, or at least unidentifiable, animals. It is thought that some of these strange animals are representations of humans acting like animals, thus their forms are difficult to interpret. They could also be representations of ogres or other fictional beings. Animal tracks are also prevalent, some of which are easy to identify such as sand hill crane, crow, and ungulate tracks. Plants also feature prominently with representations of corn stalks and evergreen trees along with other less easily identified plants.

Geometric or abstract forms are common in addition to representative forms with circles, spirals, zig-zags, and wavy lines occurring in large numbers. There are also triangles, stars, sets of concentric rings, curvilinear forms, and step-like designs. Small crossed lines or sets of arrows may represent celestial bodies, like stars or planets, or perhaps something else that we don't understand. The Chaco Culture was quite adept at astronomy and had many significant building features and shrines that aligned to obvious celestial events like equinoxes and solstices. The most famous Chaco astronomical device is a spiral carved into a cliff face on Fajada Butte such that it acts like a celestial calendar. A thin knife of sunlight, shining through an adjacent gap in a rock, traces the

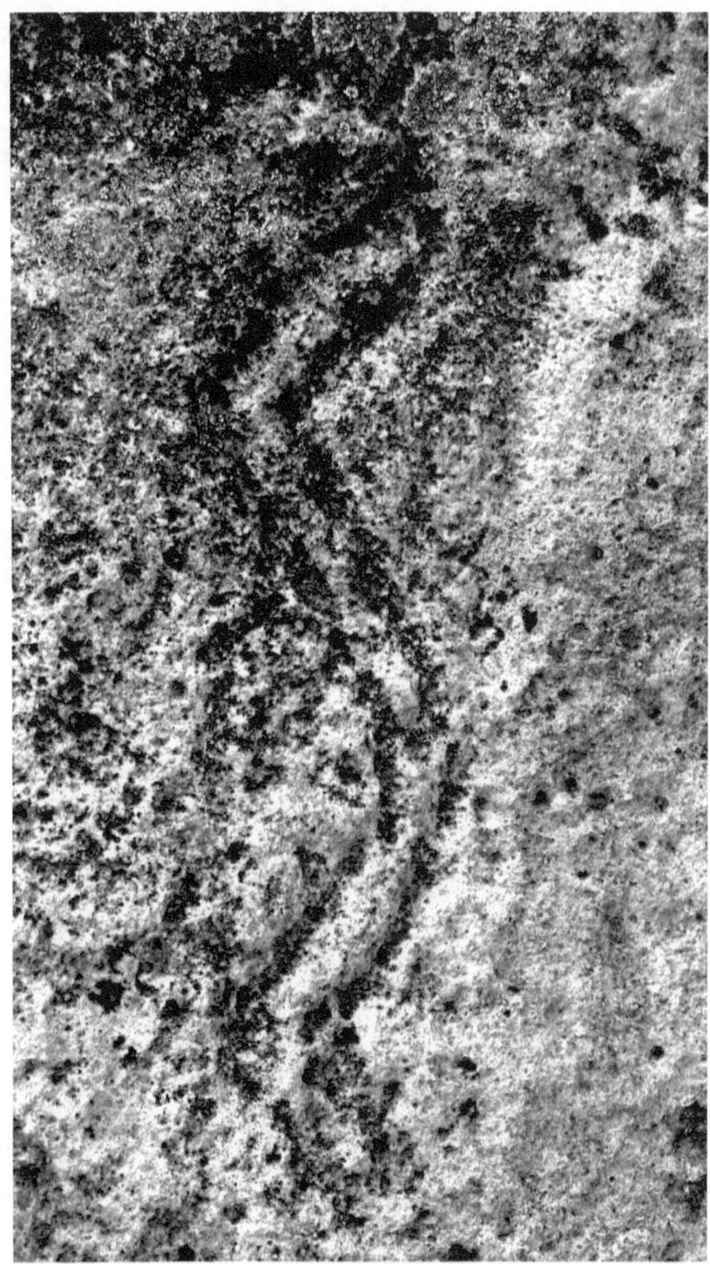

A pair of zig-zags running rughly parallel.

Above: Several geometric forms and a large curvelinear form.

Below : A trapezoidal form inside of a roughly circular form.

spiral and indicates important astronomical events such as the summer solstice. Some of this astronomical understanding surely would have passed down to the Tsankawi residents and thus been represented in petroglyphs. There is also at least one human hand-print that has been carved out, perhaps as a signature or to convey a prayer. Overall, differing sets of motifs have been found to be associated with physical features of the community and with types of dwellings. There is a set of motifs associated with quarries that is entirely separate from the set found near water control features like dams and irrigation systems. Yet another set of motifs is prevalent near farming locations. The site specificity of the types of motifs used further supports the idea of a proto-lingual or contextual information carrying capacity for the art.

One thing that comparative analysis of petroglyphs has provided is another layer of differentiation between the north and south ends of the plateau. Art placement and motif categories clearly diverge between Tsankawi and Frijoles Canyon, for instance. Contrasts between artwork styles strongly suggests that there was a cultural and linguistic divide between the ends of the plateau, consistent with that seen in pottery style. Art researchers call this divide a north-south semantic boundary.

Unfortunately, there are also a few forgeries, or examples of vandalism, at the site. These are easily recognized as more recent carving because they exhibit no signs of weathering or lichen growth, the forms are not consistent with the aesthetic of the rest of the carvings, and they were clearly made with a much sharper, probably metal, carving implement. Their thinner, more exact lines are obviously not made with the same types of tools as the original carvings. It should go without saying that these are in poor taste and that modern peoples should not attempt to add to, or upstage, the ancient carvings as a matter of general respect to the ancient people, or at least to the Park Service. I have not included any images of the vandalism so as not to encourage vandals with publicity. In contrast to obvious vandalism, a few new carvings have appeared at other ancient Puebloan sites since archeologists first documented them. These new carvings are consistent with the style and aesthetic of the ancient carvings and seem to have been produced in an authentic manner. It is possible that some petro-glyph sites, though probably not Tsankawi, are actively maintained and used for ongoing ceremonial purposes by modern Puebloans, despite the fact that the sites are not permanently inhabited.

Trails, a cavate, and a staircase on the south side of Tsankawi Mesa.

End of Occupation and Cultural Affiliations

The prevailing theory as to why the Tsankawi inhabitants left the village is that a drought right around the turn of the 16th to the 17th century made the area around the mesa unsuitable for agriculture. Residents were forced to leave for locations with better access to water, such as the pueblos closer to the Rio Grande. There is no permanent water source near the mesa at the present, lending credibility to this idea. Contact with the Spanish invaders at roughly the same time period may also have contributed. The Spanish founded nearby Santa Fe in 1607, but had been settling in other areas several years earlier. Where exactly the Tsankawi residents ended up is the subject of some debate, with little physical evidence for any theory. Tewa traditions in the San Idelfonso and Santa Clara Pueblos near Española, among others, say that they are descended directly from upland villagers living at Tsankawi, Tsirege, Otowi, Puye, and other sites on the northern end of the plateau. The Santa Clara Pueblo successfully gained legal control over the cliff dwellings at Puye based partly on their own traditional history and partly on historical agreements made with the Spanish. Similar traditions in the Cochiti Pueblo, south of Santa Fe, hold that the Tyuonyi village at Frijoles Canyon and other related sites are their direct ancestral homes. In the past it was common for archeologists and anthropologists to discount oral histories and cultural traditions when assigning ancestry to Pueblos and their inhabitants. A treatment of Bandelier from the 1950s, by Hewett, which is factually quite rich otherwise, gives a fairly scathing refutation of the local lore as nearly completely false citing what he saw as a clear and abrupt disconnect between the cultures of Bandelier and the surrounding modern Pueblos. In the 1920s, several prominent archeological figures completely discounted oral tradition as "biased" and "unreliable" in a similar fashion. Essentially, the scientific standard of the first half of the 20th century was to ignore tradition and oral history in favor of European-American theory and extrapolation based on scant evidence.

More recent researchers have been paying attention to what the Puebloans have to say about themselves. Some stories, when examined next to recent hard archeological evidence, have turned out to be quite credible. One example of a validated oral history comes form Cochiti Pueblo. Different oral historians, speaking Keres and living in or around Cochiti Pueblo, have told similar stories in several overlapping versions over the years about how the group once resided at Tyuonyi in what is now Bandelier National Monument. According to the general outline of the differing versions, prior to the arrival of Europeans, and due to vague or unnamed problems, different groups of people moved out of Frijoles Canyon in different directions at different times. Their immediate destinations included the Pueblo of the Stone Lions, Santo Domingo Pueblo, Hanat Kotyiyi, and a few other nearby locations. There are intermediate steps in the story, but ultimately the different emigration groups retained similar culture and languages and collectively engaged in conflict with the Spanish when they arrived in the area. The Spanish prevailed and forcibly moved them to their current Keres speaking Pueblos where they still reside. Archeological evidence and historical records from the Spanish conquistadors have confirmed the general timeline of occupation at the named locations in the story. Inventing a fictitious or disingenuous timeline of events to support the claim that Cochiti Pueblo residents are descended from Tyuonyi and later have that timeline randomly match the scientific facts on the ground would be extremely difficult. The easier and simpler explanation is that the oral histories of Cochiti Pueblo are truthful and fairly accurate portrayals of the past.

In light of the validation of the Cochiti Pueblo traditions, there is no reason to believe that at least some of the residents of the modern Tewa pueblos to the north are not descended from the northern Pajarito villages, including Tsankawi, as their histories claim. As mentioned briefly earlier, the pottery types found at Tsankawi and surrounding sites, as well as the style of the petroglyphs, seem to point to at least a linguistic or cultural relationship between the Tewa speaking pueblos and the northern Pajarito villages.

One factor to consider in the search for ancestry is how the contemporary pueblos would have functioned in the very late Classic Period, sometimes called the Riverine Period, just before Spanish contact. It is referred to as the Riverine because major population centers were (and still are) predominantly in low-lying areas near consistent year-round water sources, such as the Rio Grande River. In contrast, Chaco Canyon's Chaco Wash only carried water seasonally, even at the zenith of Chacoan power. Taos, Santa Clara, San Idelfonso, Tesuque, Nambé, Pojoaque, Picuris, and many other modern pueblos are classic examples of the Riverine Pueblo. The Riverine pueblos originally controlled strips of territory that extended from the river uphill to the summits of the nearest adjacent mountain range. The advantage to the river-to-peak approach was that each community had access to small parts of many differing ecosystems, instead of controlling a large portion of any one zone. The Rio Grande runs through mixed juniper grasslands, the Pajarito has piñon-juniper scrub woodland in the canyons with montane ponderosa forests on the higher mesas, and the peaks of the Valles Caldera reach all the way into the subalpine zone with forests of predominantly fir and spruce. The only nearby ecosystems not represented in this strip are desert and alpine tundra (though alpine tundra can be found on Redondo peak inside the caldera), neither of which are especially helpful for survival. A diverse territory yielded more hunting and foraging opportunities to supplement agriculture and allowed easy access to timber and mineral resources for construction and tools.

Santa Clara Pueblo, or Kha'po Owingeh, was built around 1550 and is a good example of the Riverine paradigm. The modern reservation, after the aforementioned recent legal reconquest of the Puye Cliffs, is a long narrow stretch of land running west from the Rio Grande up to the Valles Caldera, passing through the Pajarito Plateau in between. This rough area is likely somewhat similar to the original pre-Spanish holdings. San Idelfonso Pueblo, or P'ohwhóge Owingeh meaning, "where the water cuts through" in Tewa, was originally established around 1300. In the Riverine period it likely controlled a long strip of land just to the south of Santa Clara's territory, similarly stretching from the Rio Grande to the Valles Caldera. Tsankawi and several other ruins are situated directly along this strip of land, inside the San Idelfonso sphere of Riverine influence. In the 21st century the San Idelfonso reservation stretches only up to the edge of modern Los Alamos and the National Laboratory, which reside on the plateau directly between the pueblo at the river and the Caldera. They cut off the reservation and prevent it from reaching the peaks. Tsankawi is directly adjacent to the western extent of San Idelfonso's reservation land, and is sandwiched between the reservation and Lab property that would have originally been included in the Riverine strip. The fact that Santa Clara's and San Idelfonso's river-to-peak Riverine territories would have naturally incorporated the major ruined villages of the northern Pajarito sites under the Riverine paradigm, lends another layer of credibility to their views that these ruins are the homes of their ancestors.

There is some evidence, including linguistic evidence, that a portion of the population in the upper Rio Grande region may be from outside of New Mexico, but it does not fully discount the possibility of at least partial descent from the Pajarito area. The linguistic evidence cited is that Tewa, along with Towa, and Tiwa, is a Kiowa-Tanoan language. Kiowa-Tanoan languages, as the name suggests, are a combination of Kiowa, a language originally spoken in Kansas, Oklahoma, and Texas, and Tanoan. Tanoan is the collective name for Tiwa, Tewa, and Towa. On a side note, all those state names where Kiowa or related languages are spoken are of Native American origin, but none are from a Kiowa-Tanoan language. Oklahoma is a Choctaw word meaning "red people" referring Native Americans generally, Kansas is the name of a tribe also known as Kaw, and Texas is a Caddo word meaning "friends." The linguistic relationship of Kiowa to the Tanoan languages may point to an influx of Midwesterners into the area at some juncture in the distant past but is not conclusive proof of any genetic relationship one way or another.

Direct genetic evidence may be able to sort out the relationships between modern pueblos and ancient ones to a degree that would be universally accepted by archeology. Unfortunately, no major genetic study has ever been undertaken on a widespread basis among Pueblo peoples, so there is no concrete way to decide the precise biological relationship between groups of people. It is my understanding that most Pueblo people are not interested in proving anything to science that they know inherently as a community. To make a vague and sweeping statement about many different groups of people is risky, but it seems that Puebloans are resistant to the idea of genetic testing, especially on the remains of their ancestors, but also on themselves. Someday the questions about migration and inheritance may be able to be answered more completely and scientifically, but at this point, in light of the ceramic, artistic, and territorial evidence, I think it is unwise to completely discount what the modern Puebloan peoples have to say about themselves and their ancestors.

Preservation

Tsankawi is technically an active archeological research site, despite its many visitors each year and lack of current excavation or research. While we do know a lot about the site, there is much more that we do not know. Further excavation is necessary to fully understand the ruins, yet as time passes information is slowly being lost due to weathering, vegetation incursion, animal activity, and most painfully, human activity. Preservation of the site for further research is an ongoing issue with several challenging aspects including freeze-thaw cycles, accidental human damage, and intentional human damage. The site is important for archeologists and anthropologists as well as Tewa-speaking peoples who have a cultural connection to the buildings, shrines, artwork, and artifacts. Since the 1990s, almost all of the academic and institutional energy expended on Tsankawi has been put toward assessing past damage and planning for the mitigation of future damage, rather than the collection of new archeological or cultural data. The Park Service and the University of Pennsylvania have actively worked with San Idelfonso Pueblo on the issues surrounding the preservation of Tsankawi. Several academic papers, graduate theses, and internal Park Service reports were written about the management and preservation of cultural resources at Bandelier, or Tsankawi in particular, between 1998 and 2009. They all tend to agree that there are problems and that more could be done to intervene.

Among the unknowns about Tsankawi are the exact locations and nature of the expected village shrines. Tewa associated sites always have directional shrines as well as other ritual or ceremonial shrines scattered around the village. Many of the expected shrines for Tsankawi have never been located or excavated. There is a strong likelihood that they once existed, but they have not been found, cataloged, excavated, and documented. It is also highly likely that even innocent foot traffic may be destroying (or have already destroyed) the remaining evidence for them. It may also happen, in the worst case, that artifact hunters have intentionally looted them already.

Foot traffic at the site is often described as the most destructive factor affecting the cultural resources. The ancient Tsankawi trail system is the most visually striking and unique feature of the mesa, but has potentially fared the worst under modern visitation. The official Park Service trail loop around the mesa currently crosses over the corner of the pueblo ruin, so that you are walking on and through the walls. It is unclear why, on a barren mesa top, the trail would need to directly cross or enter any part of the pueblo as this wears on the ruin in an preventable way. In the past the official trails also ran through the centers of kivas, though some sections of the trail have been moved within the past 20 years to route around kivas out of respect for their ceremonial and spiritual nature. Aside from the official loop, many unofficial trails or regularly used alternative routes alongside the ancient trails compound the damage. In some cases the shortcuts and unofficial trails are worn more deeply than the intended loop trail, causing confusion for hikers and reinforcing their injurious use. The seemingly mundane act of walking around the site is simply not good for the preservation of the ruin. Many ancient trails have been worn so deeply, some up to 6 feet, into the tuff that they have become impassible for some visitors. A secondary volunteer trail, or a straddling of the original trail, is necessary to navigate the mesa safely in these locations. Both of these options contribute to erosion and visually deface the landscape. In a few places, carefully adding fill material to the deepest parts of the trenches has stabilized the trail to some degree. Despite the efforts, the overall problem of trail erosion and landscape degradation by visitor traffic has not been fully solved. Aerial photos from the 1920s and the 1950s, included in a paper by Frank Matero, show that even in that 30-year period, early in the Nation Monument's existence, official and unofficial trails took a large toll on the top of the mesa and the pueblo ruins. 70 years on, the situation has only worsened. Increased signage, raised walkways, or barriers have been suggested to curb the problem, though detractors say that signs or walkways would ruin the aesthetic of the site.

Signs are clearly posted at the trailhead calling Tsankawi

an "outdoor museum" and banning the collection or disturbance of artifacts such as tools or pottery shards, also called potsherds. Many people actively flout this ban and collect or move artifacts from their original sites. Piles of pottery fragments can be seen all over the site that were clearly collected and deposited together on flat rocks or in clearings of vegetation by tourists. Likely done under the misguided belief that they were helping in some way by gathering artifacts near the trails, this practice is actually destroying archeological evidence by removing the artifacts from their original locations. If and when archeologists examine these pieces they will no long be "in situ" and their value greatly diminished. Additionally, the scattering of pottery was sometimes done in funerary rituals throughout the southwest. Moving pieces of ceramic could be construed as tampering with graves or burial practices and is disrespectful. Superstition holds that collecting funerary potsherds is bad luck. Whether or not that is true, it is still against the rules and disrespectful to the culture and to the Park Service, and archeologically disadvantageous, to remove or relocate pottery fragments.

As mentioned earlier, some modern peoples have attempted to create their own petroglyphs at the site with modern tools. This is simply a defacement of the site in the most glaring sense. Names and rudimentary pictures have been ground into the rock walls of the mesa with sharp implements. Obviously this graffiti is detrimental to the site as it would be anywhere, ancient or modern.

The cavates on the cliffsides also fare poorly with intense modern human traffic. The openings to the caves and the floors adjacent to the entrance show heavy wear in recent years from a large number of visitors climbing in and out with backpacks, boots, cameras, and other gear. In some cases the structural integrity of the cave is in jeopardy from both human activity and from weathering. The lower caves are in a worse state than the higher caves, due to the accumulation of water runoff at the lower elevation and from use in historic times as shelters for livestock and livestock herders. The lower section of the cliff-face is not part of the official trail loop, so ongoing damage is mostly due to weathering. Cavates on the main trail loop are very susceptible to ongoing human degradation as well as weathering. Only a few cavates are intended to be entered by the general public. As with the trail system, however, nothing prevents park users from adventuring to other off-trail cavates and damaging them.

Unfortunately for the site as a static researchable archeological ruin, and as a cultural heritage site for modern Puebloans, it is also a dynamic tourist attraction. Attempting to have both an "outdoor museum" and a preserved site is a difficult task. Tsankawi has the compounding issues of a lack of official presence, relaxed management, and inadequate signage. In its detached state from the main section of Bandelier, it does not have much Park Ranger presence on site. This is both great for the visitors in that it is often possible to visit the site at an off-peak time and enjoy it in solitude, and bad for the site in that poor behavior by a minority of users is often unchecked. High visitation and low official presence allow for a lot of unsupervised use. Ignorance or willful violation is largely unchecked and thus damage and degradation are an ongoing issue. In the past, park officials were under the impression that visitation to the Tsankawi site was very low and, in fact, so low as to not be noteworthy. This was in direct contrast to the opinions of many archeologists and cultural resource management experts. Careful tracking from 2000-2012 showed that visitation to Tsankawi fluctuated between a low of 6,250 people in 2008 to a high of 12,297 in 2011. For context, the main section of Bandelier reported numbers in the hundreds of thousands over this same time period.

According to the academic research of the late 1900s and early 2000s, a major act of mitigation that the Monument staff could engage in is the installation of more signage. Better marking of the official trail loop and more educational signage about the site, and about the damage that visitors can potentially cause, would be extremely helpful. Another early suggestion was to remove some vegetation from the ruin so it can be better observed and to mitigate root damage to the ruins. Native vegetation could also be added in strategic places to block access to unofficial trails or to parts of the ruins that are most vulnerable to damage.

The opinion of the Park Service appears to have changed

since the initial conservation assessment work was done and for the last 5 years they have been actively planning changes at Tsankawi. A proposal was put forward in 2014 by the National Park Service to adjust some of the infrastructure to improve accessibility and address some of the preservation concerns as well as update the visitor experience. A couple of differing, yet similar, alternatives were proposed. Some of the suggested physical improvements included: adjusting the adjacent roadway for safer entry and exit with dedicated turn lanes, building a new parking area, opening a new section of trail to guided tours only, mechanically or electronically measuring visitation levels, and enhancing signage and other interpretation opportunities. Operational improvements under the proposal included the monitoring and documentation of: material loss at handholds and footholds on ancient staircases, general trail conditions, geohazards, cavate conditions, standing masonry conditions, and trailside vegetation. Also under this proposal there is a phased set of trail improvements that would reroute the main loop trail around the pueblo room blocks to the south through an area with less artifact scatter to disturb. This segment could potentially have a barrier to keep visitors from wandering off-trail. A couple of completely new sections of trail would also be added. One to take visitors farther east on the mesa top, for better views of the Sangres, and one directly to Duchess Castle from the parking area, with the option to connect to the main loop trail in the future. The existing trail to the Castle is unofficial and would be closed and reclaimed. In order to accommodate mobility-limited visitors to the extent feasible, improvements were proposed to the initial segment of trail out of the parking area. Additionally, existing but unused facilities for a site-steward would be improved so as to have a full-time employee presence at the site.

All of this potential work would address the primary preservation concerns and enhance the overall visitor experience, going above and beyond the basic recommendations of early preservation assessments. The listed upgrades require estimated capital investment between 1.3 and 1.6 million dollars with ongoing elevated maintenance and operating costs. In 2018, the National Nuclear Security Administration and the Army Corps of Engineers (the groups responsible for the safety of nuclear materials transport in and out of the National Lab) proposed a change to the intersection of East Jemez Road and NM 4, directly adjacent to the Tsankawi Unit. Among other things, this proposal would allow for turn lanes into and out of a new parking area in accordance with the Park Service's 2014 plans. As of late 2019, however, neither the road construction nor the Tsankawi update proposals have been implemented. According to Bandelier officials, the 2014 plan is their preferred course of action for the future, but it is still being considered and there has been no final approval or official timeline for the project.

One additional factor to contemplate in the overall discussion of archeological preservation and conservation is the viewpoint of native culture. The European archeological and historical need to preserve the past in physical objects and standing structures is sometimes directly at odds with the culture being studied and documented. Some Native Americans believe that preservation of an ancient site, or collection of artifacts in the style of a museum, is absurd and illogical. Ethnologist Frank Cushing ran up against significant resistance to the preservation of ruins and ancient artifacts when he was working with the Zuni people in the early 20th century. His efforts to minimize weather damage and rebuild historic sites were viewed as pointless or unnatural by the Zuni. He was reportedly told that saving a building from collapse would not revive their ancestors or change the past and was therefore not worth the effort. In the Zuni worldview, which is likely similar to that of many Puebloans, the decay of ancestral sites is a natural part of the cycle of life. Nothing lasts forever and saving objects in a pristine state, as in a museum, is not part of their cultural practice. Decisions made at Tsankawi, since the late 1990s at least, have been made with the advice of San Idelfonso Pueblo, which is certainly helping the Park Service to make informed choices. While western archeology views the ruins at Tsankawi as abandoned and empty, San Idelfonso members believe the ruin is very much alive with their ancestors.

A series of cavates on Tsankawi Mesa, a stabilizing repair has been made to one on the right side of the image.

Modern Connections

One of the great civilizations of North America, the Chacoan-Puebloan continuum is quite poorly understood and very under-discussed in America as a whole. Stretching from the Pleistocene to the present in a contiguous series of rising and falling episodes, the prehistory and history of the Southwest is worth noting. Usually for political reasons, but sometimes just out of ignorance, the pre-European civilizations and societies of North America have always been marginalized or regarded as a footnote to the rest of the world's human activities. I certainly do not remember encountering any information about the Chaco Culture in school. In most cases, no education curriculum emphasizes Native American pre-contact civilizations outside of region-specific college anthropology or archeology courses. In other words, you have to exert intentional effort to find information on Chaco and the prehistoric southwest. It is surprising to many modern American citizens that New Mexico, regarded a backwater or flyover state by most coastal city-dwellers, was home to a civilization as advanced as the Chaco phenomenon. The Mississippian culture responsible for the metropolis at Cahokia is similarly overlooked, but thanks to the large masonry buildings and the arid climate, the New Mexicans of the past left us plenty of tangible and awe-inspiring evidence for their existence and their quite impressive abilities. Under most circumstances, the Meso-American cultures, Olmec, Maya, Aztec, and others along with the Inca of South America, are taught as the only notable empires of the west. Chaco and its descendants, which are still here and living much as their ancestors did, ought to be grouped into that category of notable New World civilizations.

Disturbingly, many mentions of Chaco Canyon or Mesa Verde in popular culture, or even those few educational textbooks that make reference at all, imply that after their political decline in the 12th century the people simply vanished mysteriously into the mists of time. Some film documentaries and books (and some outdated scholarly works) even claim that the modern Puebloans are simply copycats or usurpers with no relationship to the Anasazi, whose fate is some kind of unknowable cosmic enigma. I have seen written passages in older texts insinuating that even the name of the Pueblo Period is inaccurate or a misnomer because it connects modern Pueblos to the ancient Great Houses in a way that the writers find disingenuous or somehow an erroneous extension of logic. Sites like Mesa Verde, Tyuonyi, Tsankawi, and thousands of others clearly show that an advanced culture capable of large stone building projects and complex society continued, with natural evolution and reorganization, right up to the arrival of the Spanish and through to the 21st century. The Upland, Coalition, and Classic Periods are not wholly removed from the Chaco world, but a continuation of it.

The facts clearly show that the "disappearance of the Anasazi" is no more than a myth born of ignorance and a political desire to sweep modern Puebloans under the proverbial rug of history. Those ancient people would likely have continued to prosper independently today if left to their own devices, yet the Spanish interfered in the late 16th century. Even after the Spanish took control, the Pueblo Revolt of the 17th century showed that Pueblo peoples could still organize in an unprecedented way. Puebloans are one of the only examples of an indigenous people to successfully defeat the Spanish Empire, even if that victory was only sustained for a brief time. The numerous Pueblos of modern New Mexico are perhaps not the grand region-dominating political force that the Chaco culture once was, but they are the living legacy of that culture.

Among Native American groups, the Pueblo peoples have fared relatively well against the onslaught of European colonialism. Recently, a Pueblo woman was elected to congress and many of the Pueblos have rebounded from the days of slavery and forced conversion to Catholicism with successful casinos and other businesses. Where some Native American tribes were wiped out or have completely lost their cultural identity, and others have lost their homelands (like my Choctaw ancestors), the Puebloans have pushed through and retained at least some of their culture, religion, and their physical homes. This relative success in the face of long odds, and not without significant struggle, should be celebrated in modern times as well as back through the ages. From Tsankawi and the larger Riverine lowland pueblos of the 15th and 16th centuries to Tyuonyi and other Coalition pueblos of the 14th century to Mesa Verde and the other Upland cliff dwellings of the 13th century to Pueblo Bonito and the Great Houses of the 10th-12th centuries, the original inhabitants of the region have found ways to prosper and develop a rich and civilized culture on a level that deserves much more recognition.

To sum up the Pueblo peoples, I'll paraphrase a Pueblo elder whose land overlooks the city of Albuquerque. When interviewed, the man said that his ancestors had stood there and looked down on the valley well before Europeans arrived and he was confident that his descendants would look down on it after the Europeans had gone.

Sources

Barry, Patricia. *Bandelier National Monument*. Tucson: Southwest
      Parks and Monuments Association, 1990.

Barrett, Elinore M. *Conquest and Catastrophe: Changing Rio
      Grande Pueblo Settlement Patterns in the Sixteenth and
      Seventeenth Centuries*. Albuquerque: University of
      New Mexico Press, 2002.

Castetter, Edward F. "The Vegetation of New Mexico." *New
      Mexico Quarterly*. Vol. 26, Issue 3, 1956.

Chronic, Halka. *Roadside Geology of New Mexico*. Missoula:
      Mountain Press Publishing Company, 1987.

Elliot, Michael L. "Tsankawi Preservation Project Cultural
      Resources Inventory and Site Relocation." National Park
      Service, 1999.

Hewett, Edgar L. *Pajarito Plateau and its Ancient People*.
      Albuquerque: University of New Mexico Press, 1953.

Kohler, Timothy A. Ed. *Archeology of Bandelier National
      Monument – Village Formation on the Pajarito Plateau,
      New Mexico*. Albuquerque: University of New Mexico
      Press, 2004.

Laskey, Kirsten, "East Jemez Road/NM 4 Intersection May Be
      Modified." *Los Alamos Daily Post*. November 22, 2018.

Matero, Frank G. "Exploring Conservation Strategies for
      Ancestral Puebloan Sites." *Conservation and Management
      of Archaeological Sites*. Volume 6, 2003.

Merkel, Stephen, et al. "Architectural Conservation Report -
Tsankawi Mesa Cavate Conservation Project." National
Park Service, 2008-2009.

Muldavin, Esteban and Phil A. Tonne. *Vegetation Survey and
Preliminary Ecological Assessment of Valles Caldera
National Preserve, New Mexico*. University of New
Mexico, 2003.

Noble, David Grant. *In Search of Chaco*. School of American
Research, 2004.

Powers, Robert P., Ed. *The Peopling of Bandelier – New Insights
from the Archeology of the Pajarito Plateau*. Santa
Fe: School of American Research Press, 2005.

Provencher, Shaun. "Cultural Landscape Preservations Issues:
Tsankawi Mesa, Bandelier National Monument" (1998).
University of Pennsylvania. *Theses (Historic Preservation)*.
478.

Rohn, Arthur H. *Rock Art of Bandelier National Monument*.
Albuquerque: University of New Mexico Press, 1989.

Snead, James E. "Trails of Tradition: Archaeology, Landscape, and
Movement." Lecture Notes. University of
Pennsylvania Museum, May 26-31, 2006.

Stuart, David E. *Pueblo Peoples on the Pajarito Plateau –
Archeology and Efficiency*. Albuquerque: University of
New Mexico Press, 2010.

Stuart, David E. *Anasazi America*. 2nd edition. Univeristy of New
Mexico Press, 2014.

Smith, Monica L. "The Historic Period at Bandelier National
     Monument." Intermountain Cultural Resources
     Management Professional Paper No. 63. National Park
     Service, 2002.

'Tsankawi Trail – Bandelier National Monument." Western
     National Parks Association, National Park Service.
     Pamphlet.

"Tsankawi Unit Management Plan and Environmental
     Assessment" Bandelier National Monument, National Park
     Service, October 2014.

About the Author

Ryan Alexander Bloom is a member of the Choctaw Nation of Oklahoma and a resident of New Mexico, where he frequently explores indigenous archeological sites. He has previously written 3 instructional drum books, published with Hudson Music, and holds a bachelor's degree in music from the University of Colorado. This is Ryan's first non-musical publication, for which he also did all of the photography, layout, graphic design, and editing.